WILLIAM E DOWELL

Biography

WILLIAM E DOWELL

PAGE PUBLISHING, INC.
New York, NY

First originally published by Page Publishing, Inc. 2016

ISBN 978-1-68348-030-3 (pbk)
ISBN 978-1-68348-031-0 (digital)

Printed in the United States of America

ACKNOWLEDGMENTS

Thanks to Dr. Jessica K. Dowell Brown and Lydia Greene and Nathanial Phillips for making this book a success.

AUTHOR'S NOTE

This biography of William E. Dowell are the facts given to me by my parents and others. I've revealed the truth, which tells of those whom I came to know as a child and as an adult and how, as a child, we met while in the huts and after we crossed paths growing up in St. Louis, Missouri.

If the truth hurts, too bad; it's what happened. Every young person should read this; it may help them avoid some of the pitfalls I endured in life.

DOWELL NAMED VP

William E. Dowell Jr. has been named regional vice president of marketing for National Prearranged Services Inc. located at 10 S. Brentwood in Clayton, Missouri. Mr. Dowell has been appointed to this position by James Crawford, CEO of the corporation.

Mr. Dowell will be responsible for recruiting, field training, and servicing funeral homes in Missouri, Illinois, and Texas. NPS is a nationwide marketing firm engaged in the business of helping families in prearranging their funerals. It is NPS's mission to see that every family in America has adequate information along the choices that are available to them when death occurs. NPS is a consumer-oriented company and is very active in promoting legislation for consumer protection.

Prior to joining NPS, Mr. Dowell enjoyed the position of president of William Dowell Inc., the first black-owned wholesale liquor wine distributor in the state of Missouri in 1974. Mr. Dowell hired and trained the first black woman to be allowed to sell alcoholic beverages. Mr. Dowell, together with the law firm of Bussy, Collier, and Dorsy, broke the barriers through suits filed with EEOC, allowing black salesmen and saleswomen to sell to the chain stores in territory litigation. He was also the owner of Butter Rump Tripe Restaurants.

Dowell received his BS degree from St. Louis University and attended the master's program at Southern Illinois University. He graduated from Aetna University Insurance Institute, Hartford, Connecticut. Mr. Dowell served twelve years in the United States Marine Corps. He is a Vietnam veteran and received the Purple Heart twice, as well as meritorious mass for bravery in the face of the enemy in Da Nang, South Vietnam. Dowell was the first ward Republican committeeman for eight years and city chairman for the Robert Dole Republican Campaign for President Committee. Dowell made an unsuccessful bid for state representative in the Fifty-First District against Paula Carter.

Mr. Dowell is currently a volunteer for the Missouri Department of Probation and Parole, coaches basketball for Mathews-Dickey Boys' & Girls Club and the Bethel and Central City Lutheran Schools, and he teaches golf.

PROLOGUE

It's a cold night in December. My age is sixty-six. The book is about my life living in St. Louis, education, love, and those whom I've known for years, from the age of five. I can remember the huts, a low-income housing for veterans' families. This is about the lives of individuals whom I will meet the first and the second time as an adult. The names and incidents are true, and those mentioned come from the memories from childhood till now.

MY PEOPLE

I'll list names, and throughout the book, I will associate the names with particular events in my life.

- Myrdell Dowell—Josie
- Candy Baby
- Jerry Parker, Mel Joe Franklin
- Tiny Parker, Scezie Franklin
- Floyd Lee Turner, Barbara Ann Franklin
- Earlene Turner, Earl Strout
- Jackie Brown, James Harper
- Paul Brown, Jerry Harper
- Lorraine Brown
- Melvin Harper
- Joe Grimes Sr., Andry Rose
- Joe Grimes Jr.
- Robert Battle
- Marva Grimes
- Beatrice Battle
- Robert Simpson, Early Kelly
- Elaine Williams
- Freddie Washington
- Roger Williams
- Ralph Washington
- Clyde Earl
- Butch the Dog.
- Clifford Sledge

- Sylvia Beckwith
- Gail Sledge (Lynn Sledge)
- Peggie Beckwith
- Peddie Washington, Marsha Beckwith
- Rolene Washington, Eunice Beckwith
- Carla Washington, Veronica Jones
- Ronald Pace, Brenda Kelly
- Beverly Pace, Odell Douglas
- Laura—Lenord
- Emma Mitchell
- Alvine Lenord, Roy Junior
- Babe Lenord
- Emanuel Bryant
- Louis Raymond
- Leroy Pankins
- Melvin Raymond
- John Pankins, Calvin Raymond
- Be Bee, Swazie Raymond
- Ronald Johnson, Sylvester Raymond
- Goldie Sutton, Billy Earl White
- Joyce Tankins, Molly Witmore
- Harvey Raspberry, "Trouble" Lavere Whitmore
- Delmar Raspberry
- Deborah Raspberry
- Lottie M. Martin Hargrove, Solacon Thurmon Moore
- Pam McCollough, Marciano Greene Sr.
- Johnnie McCollough, Marciano Greene Jr.
- Bernice McCollough, Leslie Green
- Simon Ward Val Teeter
- Nathanial Phillips
- Terry Fisher Marshall
- Laura Marion
- Tammy Marshall, Ann Phillips
- Butch Marshall, Joe Reg Thomas—Louella Thomas
- Betty Aldrich, Youel Thomas
- Ina Dennis, Jerry Warren

- Lozanza Dennis, Akins Warren
- Sonya Dennis, Jimmy Warren
- Rosland Dennis, Walter Warren
- Lloyd Browner, Mary Warren
- Joyce Browner
- Leolan Browner
- Amon Evens, Ron McIntyre
- Emery Evans, Ed James
- Joe Mayfill, Ivan James
- Ollie Mayfill, James Buford
- Theodore Edwards, Ronald Ford
- Sandra Scott, Dewitt Billinley
- Marvin Scott, Vinnie Lions
- Marvin Boone, Carl Davis
- Monrow, Blackmon
- Lavert Trotter, Julius Kirkscy
- Deelin Kelly, Elbert Dorsy
- Rosland Kelly, Charles Bussey
- Flim Thomas, OJ
- Tessie Thomas
- Anthony Hamilton, Jaunita Hamilton
- Oscar Lee Middlebrook, policeman, detective
- Mary Ezell, Lorazon McWright
- Oliver Ezell, Patricia Grime
- Vincent Wright, Carl Cameron
- Robert Cole, Bubby Cameron
- Sue Roberts
- Michael Pricie (Conrad Ingram)
- Kenneth Shead
- Bruce Shead
- Robert Marley
- Ronald Marley
- Bobby Vally
- Dorthy Vally
- Cliff Baker, Herbert Gardner
- Eddie Baker, Roy Dean—Rail Head

- Archie Wayne, Cynthia Edwards
- Earl Harvey, Odessa Harris
- John El, Gladys Pierce
- Gluche, John Warren
- Ecka Patterson Spears
- Earl James Smith
- Hawitha Moore, Leslie McCall
- Willamae Moore, Bruce Smith—Boody
- Verdell Lewis, John Smith
- Fred Lewis, Normon James
- Baby Baby Lewis, Jackie Sanders
- Frank, Lula Bardoux
- Lucille Shelton Washington, Fillis Foxwell
- Orchie Washington, Andrew Bell
- Eldridge Bryant, Barry Tellphie
- Lillian Foster
- Ethel Foster, Barbara Porter
- Oliver Lake, Birlinda Davis
- Pat McLomore, Marilyn Green
- Newton Troope—Alvin Troope
- Betty Fisher
- Johnny McGrew, Eugene Taylor Bean
- Robert Franklin, Richard Taylor
- Dorry Bolden, Nathaniel Taylor—Rollo
- La val Bolden, Hugh Davis
- Tim Normon, Ronald Jones
- James Dyson
- Marlean Hampton
- Ricky Hampton
- Marvin Neals
- Betty Dowell
- James Conwell
- James Hopson
- Sophie
- Nathanial Corn
- Wanda Morgonfield

- Larry Davis
- Julius Kirksey
- Johnny Roland
- George Seals
- Gerald Stevenson
- Helton Reed
- Jimmy Rollins

IMPORTANT LEADERS
I'VE PERSONALLY MET

- President Lyndon B. Johnson, awarded William Dowell Purple Heart, Guam Island, MI, 1968
- Marine Commandant Wallace M. Green Jr., awarded William Dowell second Purple Heart, Guam, Mariana Islands, 1968
- Dr. Martin Luther King Jr. Airport, Washington DC, January 29, 1968
- Lee Elder, PGA golf champion. I played golf with Lee in St. Louis, Missouri, Lambs Club Tournament 1975. He bet me two dollars he could drive the PAR 4 hole 15 at Forest Park. He did; he put it on the green.
- Mike Shannon, St. Louis Cardinal. I played golf with Mike at Forest Park in Celebrity Golf Tournament 1980. Mike puts with a 3-wood, loves beer.
- Calvin Peete spent twenty-four hours with me for my birthday (9/20/1987). While he was in St. Louis, Missouri, Calvin held a golf clinic sponsored by Coca-Cola Bottling Company at Bellerive Country Club. I picked up Calvin Peete at the Ritz-Carlton Hotel at 6:00 p.m., and he accompanied me to Daymon's Lounge in my own personal limo. Daymon announced that a PGA champion was in the house. A real down-to-earth person. God bless him. I returned accompanied him to his hotel at 3:00 a.m. and thanked him., He said he enjoyed the regular people, and we exchanged addresses. At that time, he was having a rotator cup problem with his shoulder. Talked with him on

the phone but never seen him again. Aa pro -all -the -way, a regular guy.

- Bob Tums, president of Tums for the 3 Tummy. Lake of the Ozarks, August 1985. Bob invited me to play golf with him at Ozark Country Club. I visited him at his office in St. Louis downtown the following week. Told me to call him so we could play again.
- Ivory Crockett, the fastest human from Alton, Illinois, played in a golf tournament in St. Louis, May 1980, Forest Park. Sponsored by Paramount Golf Club. We played these holes together that day with Mike Shonnon.
- General William C. Westmorland, commanding army general of Vietnam War 1966. I was wounded November 12, 1966, in Vietnam. I was medevac to U.S. Army hospital in the Philippines for surgery. The general stayed in my hospital room, waiting for hours for me to awaken. The doctor told me that the general slept in that chair, waiting for me to wake up because he wanted to hear from me what happened at Antrack, Vietnam, when we got overrun by the Viet Cong.
- Red Skelton. Las Vegas, June 1972. I met Red and had a picture taken with him at the Sands Hotel. We had a drink together. He said he was buying. You know, drinks in Vegas are free while gaming. Funny man.
- Frank Sinatra, Las Vegas, June 1972.
- Sammie Davis Jr., Las Vegas, June 1972. I gambled with them at the Sands Hotel on the crap table. I lost, Sammie talked, and Junk didn't say much. I didn't ask for an autograph.

PERSONAL TRAVEL

- Denver, Colorado
- Tijuana, Mexico
- Colorado Springs
- Washington, DC
- Las Vegas
- Baltimore, Maryland
- San Francisco
- Cape Canaveral, Florida
- San Diego, California
- Springfield, Illinois
- Los Angeles, California
- Evansville, Illinois
- Ft. Wayne, Texas
- Nashville, Tennessee
- Chicago, Illinois
- Paducah, Kentucky
- Indianapolis, Indiana
- Kansas City, Missouri
- Dayton, Ohio
- Biloxi, Mississippi
- Louisville, Kentucky
- Jackson, Mississippi
- Memphis, Tennessee
- Tunica, Mississippi
- Chattanooga, Tennessee
- Tupelo, Mississippi

- Atlanta, Georgia
- Vancleave, Mississippi
- Houston, Texas
- New York, New York
- New Orleans, Louisiana
- Charleston, North Carolina
- Ft. Lauderdale, Florida
- Jacksonville, South Carolina
- Miami, Florida
- Morehead City, South Carolina
- Pensacola, Florida
- Raleigh, South Carolina
- Jackson, Tennessee
- Toledo, Ohio
- Palm Springs, California
- Richmond, Virginia
- Oceanside, California
- Milwaukee, Wisconsin
- Orlando, Florida
- Detroit, Michigan
- Canada
- Lake Erie
- San Juan, Puerto Rico
- Cancun, Mexico
- Puerto Vallarta, Mexico
- Honolulu, Hawaii
- Guam, Mariana Islands
- Saipan, Mariana Islands
- Vietnam
- Nassau, Bahamas
- Key West, Florida
- Freeport, Bahamas
- New Zealand
- Philippines
- Japan
- Manitoba

Huts 2841, Magazine, St. Louis, Missouri. Same
as recruit huts, San Diego, California.

CHAPTER 1

The huts were Quonset huts painted army green. Bordered by Magazine, Glasgow, Leffingwell, and Elliot Streets. They covered a four-block area in the city of St. Louis, Missouri. To the best of my knowledge, there were twenty-five Quonset huts in the area. A pavilion called the Bandstand was in the middle of the complex. Those prefabricated, corrugated metal huts were so hot in the summertime we would have to sleep outside on blankets. Most people didn't have fans.

The huts measured approximately twenty-four feet wide and seventy-five feet long. The half-moon-shaped building had two low windows on either side. There used to be a television show, *Gomer Pile Show*, which portrayed military units. Those living quarters were the same huts that I lived in. Divide that seventy-five-foot length in half because two families were in the building, one in the front and one in the back.

With no back door and only side window, a fire could have been very tragic. It would have affected not just my family but the Franklins, Odie, and Hattie in the back half with Mel Joe, Scezie, and Barbara Ann. There were six other families to the west of us on Magazine: the Turners, Floyd Lee (son), and Earlene (daughter); Odie and Hattie Franklin; Mel Joe, Scezie, Barbara Ann; the Browns, Jackie, Paul, and Lorraine; the Grimes, Joe, Marva, and Gary.

Next door to the Grimes was a little boy named Harvey. Since he was not my age, I didn't know too much about his family. Next to little Harvey, there was the Lloyd Simpson family, with Sarah,

Robert, and Joyce. We were friends. Mr. Simpson and my father had the same yellow-and-black 1954 Mercury.

All the families on Magazine looked out for one another. If one of the children did something wrong, someone always saw it. So you got a whipping from the neighbor. Then the neighbor took you home to explain what happened. Your second whipping came from your parents. Even though we were always safe, the kids weren't real happy with that good-neighbor practice.

As you entered the living room area on the right, the kitchen area (cabinets on one wall) on the left was open with enough for a table and four chairs. Past the living room / kitchen area was a hall closet (the only closet) with the bathroom across from it having only a shower. In the back were two bedrooms large enough for a double bed, a dresser, and a small chair. It was pretty tight quarters.

CHAPTER 2

We lived at 2841 Magazine. The Parkers, Whity and Maggie, Jerry (son) and Tiny (daughter), lived east of us on the corner. They had the first death, Mrs. Mattie, I was exposed to. She died at the early age of twenty. My mother, Obine, would bring her food during her illness. I was so young I didn't understand her dying. The last death up the hill where the Simpsons lived was Joyce. She was our age. I can still see her in that casket of the Kunce Funeral Home on Grand.

Still, the huts were fun because every hut had children. So there was always someone to play with.

We were one of the first families to get a television. It was called a Raytheon with a small screen. TV went off at 9:00 p.m. and on at 9:00 a.m. Our house would be full of children to see *Howdy Doody Time*. Eventually everyone had a TV.

CHAPTER 3

My life all started with my parents, Willie E. Dowell and Obine Marion. They met when my mother was sixteen and attended Vashon High School. Her uncle Rad Williams brought her to St. Louis from Mississippi to live with her aunt Essie Gregory on Howard Street. My father came to St. Louis from Covington, Tennessee. He had to leave in a hurry. His father, Murry Dowell, and his uncle Willie raised my father. His mother, Ollie Coleman, lived in St. Louis with her husband, James Coleman. Dad was left in Tennessee by Ollie.

Willie Dowell Sr. got Lula Mae pregnant and was living with her mother and brother on Mr. Charlie's land and sharecropping. Willie and Lula Mae were young. Dad worked in the field and was paid in food and a little cash. One night, Lula's brother and Dad had a fight over a piece of chicken. He beat up Willie and kicked him in the ass. He told him to get away from the house and to not come back. Her brother was a man. Dad was just a kid with a family on the way. Dad went to stay with his uncle Willie down the road from Lula's house.

The following Saturday at a ball game in town, my dad waited for his brother-in-law with a two by four. When he showed up, Willie hit him in the front of his head. The two by four had laid him out. The man was in a coma, and the high sheriff was gunning for Willie Dowell. Willie hid in the woods until some people from St. Louis were going back home. He hitched a ride. Willie's first child, Betty Dowell, was born. Dad got a job at Swift packing company on Chouteau Avenue. My father was a handsome tall man with freckles on his face. He always had a new car and money. I'm his son, and I look like him and inherited some of his ways.

Willie was visiting his relatives on Howard Street across from my mother's house. That's the way they met. Obine said she liked men with new cars and money. She was seventeen and going to Vashon High School. She admitted that she was fast and hot. They hooked up, and Obine left home and told her aunt Esse that she was in Chicago with her sister Vera.

In reality, she was with Willie in a rented room downtown. Obine was pregnant with my sister Josie. They moved on the south side on Hickory not too far from Ollie Coleman. Ollie would keep Josie for Mother. They moved to the 4000 Enright and rented from Ben Thomas, who wrote the *Whirl* paper. That paper told on those who were in trouble with the police. It's still going strong today.

Myrdell Francis Dowell was my sister, but Ollie called her Josie. She was born on October 1, 1940. Willie was also spending time with Maggie, and she was pregnant also with my sister Shirley Dowell. She was born in February 1940. Willie was not married to anyone. But he did marry Obine in 1942. Willie tried to stay out of the military, but then he was drafted into the army on September 19, 1942.

On September 20, 1942, I was born—William E. Dowell Jr. Dad was in the service for two years. He was stationed in North Carolina, where he had another woman, Rowena. When he got discharged, he came back to St. Louis to be with his family. Dad would go to his mother's house at 3037 LaSalle to visit her and get his mail. One day, Obine left Josie with Ollie. When she returned, the mailman was there, and he gave her the mail to give to Ollie. She noticed a letter addressed to Willie from Rowena in North Carolina. All hell broke out between Obine, Willie, and Ollie. They got through it with Obine, but she lost respect for Ollie. Rowena had been to Ollie's house to visit Willie. My father's stepmother was named Emma Dowell, and she had eight boys who lived in Tennessee.

So we moved to the huts. I was about six years old, and I went to Curtis School for about a year. My mother worked at Kofman up the street on Magazine. There were always people at our house— Obine's coworkers, Willie's packinghouse gang and relatives. Ollie Coleman also had two sons besides Willie. Lee Arthur "Baby" and Effie were both in the underworld. Effie loved to drink whisky, and Baby loved to gamble. He made his living in the streets. Both of them loved Obine and looked out for her. While Willie was in the army, Obine told me she and Effie robbed the service station on Chouteau. The man liked Obine, and during that time, they had stamps for purchase of gas. She said Effie locked the attendant in the bathroom, and they operated the station, selling gas and stuff for about an hour. You see, Obine was tough too.

To make ends meet, Willie would have a poker game twice a month at the huts, and the gang from Swift and the men in the huts would go over. Obine and my aunts would barbecue and sell beer and shots of whisky. Obine would keep her money because Willie was a bad gambler; he would lose most of the money he made. It was good Willie and Baby knew the police in the Ninth District. They never had any trouble. Obine's brother Dug complained about the kids being around the gambling. So eventually Josie and I would have to go to Aunt Netty's house. I became very close to my aunt and my cousins Larry and Madallion. Sometimes they would go to the huts and spend the night. One of those times was not good for Larry.

Larry rode his bike to the huts, and Big Butch, a black German shepherd, bit him on his right leg. Butch was a terror in the huts. The dog roamed the area, and when a bitch dog was in heat, he would fight off all the other dogs. All the kids watched him.

Mrs. Franklin, who lived in the back half of our hut, had a female dog named Inky. She was a black terrier, but Big Butch managed to hang her with puppies each time she came in heat. We had a dog named Butch, white spitz with black ears. Butch didn't last long because he liked to chase cars going down the street. Little Butch would ambush cars rolling down Glasgow. I would have to go and get him out of the streets when we would let him out. We chained him, but when he got loose, he ran, and we couldn't catch him. He finally made a mistake and chased the wrong car. I watched him get hit. He was trying to bite the tires, and he got rolled over by the car. My dad went and picked him up. He was dead. He went to the trash can for pick up the next day. We cried for Butch but never had another dog in the huts.

CHAPTER 4

Obine got a job at F. W. Woolworths (the five-and-dime store) at 4119 Easton. Willie would leave for work at about 5:30 a.m., while Obine would get us off to school. We would catch the Cass bus and transfer to the Taylor bus to get to Visitation Catholic School at 1421 North Taylor.

Obine met Roosevelt Shelton while working at the dime store. Roosevelt's daughter, Lucille, came from Chicago to live with us in the huts. She was a very attractive, fine, well-built girl. Lucille worked up the street from the Coffmans huts. Since she worked nights, she would be home when we came from school. Obine got off work at 6:00 p.m. She and Earlene Turner, next-door neighbor, came home in a cab every day.

One day, Lucille took a nap and left the windows open because of the summer heat. Earlene's brother, Floyd Lee, was a known Peeping Tom. He would climb on the roofs of the huts and get into trouble. While Lucille slept, Floyd Lee climbed into the window, got in the bed, and hit her in the head, drawing blood. Dazed from the blows, she only saw his back as he ran out the front door. Even though Obine talked to Mrs. Turner and Willie wanted to get him for it, no police were called. They really couldn't prove he did it.

Inez worked with Obine at the dime store. She had a sister who lived down the hill in the huts with her nephew, Freddie and Ralph Washington. Josie and Ralph liked each other. Freddie was our base-ball coach. He would set up games to play other teams in the area. If they could catch, he would let everybody play—even girls. We had a good team. Freddie's father, Archie, would come down from Chicago to visit, and he met Lucille. Maybe because he was older he swept her off her feet. At that time, Lucille was going with a married man, Bailey, from the packinghouse. I didn't like Bailey, but it was a money thing to Lucille.

One weekend, Archie came to take Lucille, Josie, and me to our aunt in Gary, Indiana. He eventually married Lucille, and she stayed with him until he died. His son, Ralph, was killed in a car accident. I met Freddie on the golf course in Mount Vernon, Illinois, where we reminisced about the old days in the huts.

We talked about the baseball game with the Slaterry team six blocks down on St. Louis Avenue and Glasgow. We won the game, but there were some sore losers: Big Head Archie, Wayne, and Peddy got in a fight with Archie. Archie hit him in the ribs with a bat; he was hurt. We all ran for the huts. Freddie went to tell Gluche and John El, who were part of the Conrad gang hanging out on Madison.

Peddy and I played cowboys. We would ride sticks (make-believe horses) that we would get out of the Dumpster at the Hussman Company on Leffingwell. We all had play guns with the holster. Peddy had two guns. He would make a shooting sound, and I would say, "You missed." Peddy never would die.

Ellis McMurty, "June Bug," lived next door to Peddy. June Bug was some kin to the Franklins, who lived in the back of us. Ellis and I were good friends at De Andreis High School. He was an excellent football halfback. He was fast, and he would tackle. He ended up marrying his love, Dorothy, from high school. She became a judge. Peddy owns a car wash on Natural Bridge and Fair with his son. We are still good friends.

Next door to Freddie's hut were the Beckwiths (Sylvia, Junior, Eunice, Marsha, and Peggy—so fine). They all attended Summer High. Peggie married Dr. Taylor and became a doctor here in St. Louis. Eunice and I became friends during the junior college days. I had a crush on the beautiful green-eyed brown girl, whom I still run into every now and then.

CHAPTER 5

Elaine Williams was kin to Clifford Sledge. They were cousins. Elaine was very good friends with James Harper. James and I would cross paths later in life. Clyd Earl lived down the hill. The only thing I can remember about him was that he was good with bikes. If there was anything wrong with a bike, he could fix it. I've only seen him once since the huts.

Across from the Beckwith lived Major and Odell Douglas and Emma Mitchell, her sister. Emma came from Louisiana. She went to summer with my sister Betty. Betty moved with us from Tennessee. Willie often went to Tennessee to see his people. Obine would give parties for the girls. Floyd Lee was older than us. He worked at Hi Wills Tavern around on Madison. It was owned by Hawatha Moore and his wife, Willie Mae. It was the place where the people downtown would meet. Hawatha cut hair, and Willie Mae did hair at their shop on Madison and Glasgow. They were good people. Obine worked at their tavern later on.

Willie Mae's brother, Verdell Lewis, opened up the Hi Wills Snack Shop. He made a name for himself selling tripe. He did so well he had a home built on Lindell Avenue near Forest Park. Dr. Helen Nash lived down the street from Verdell. Willie Mae and Obine partied together. Hawatha and Willie would hunt and fish together. Even though I was young, they would take me hunting sometimes.

Obine and Willie had problems because both were seeing other people. Obine had cousins in East Saint Louis, Illinois, who were professionals. Bonny was a nurse, and Lovie was a schoolteacher. While she was over there partying with her cousins, Obine met Hampton

Russell, a married man. He owned two taverns and a liquor store. Her cousins would pick her up, and Hampton would drop her off around the corner from our hut.

Willie was told about her drop-off place, and one night, he waited for her. He whipped her, and she fell back and hit her head on the curb. She was out of it. Willie called her sister Nettie and told her what happened.

My grandmother, Laura Marion, came to St. Louis with her son, Uncle Buddy, from Mississippi. They were mad at my father. Obine took a month to recover.

After that, Willie never stayed at home much. He would leave early and come home late. They still argued, but Obine would fix his breakfast at 5:00 a.m. And every morning, Willie would play a record called *Dust My Broom*.

My sister Betty got sick. My father took her to Tennessee to her mother. Willie returned home a week later. We came home from school, and the TV was gone, and so was Willie. He left town again with Emma Mitchell. They were only in Milwaukee for four months. Emma came back pregnant. Obine was hurt. All her girlfriends would come over to console her.

No one knew that Willie had taken my sister Betty to Tennessee and she was pregnant. Mr. Turner, who lived next door to us in the huts, had a brother, Eddie. He was the father of Betty's baby. She took us all by surprise. Willie was mad, but the skillet couldn't talk about the pot.

Obine loved Willie, but he was gone. She tried to get him back by letting him stay over some nights. One day, she told him not to come back. We eventually moved from the huts to 4056 Evans. I missed all my friends in the huts. I got over it and saw some of them in later years.

CHAPTER 6

My new home was in a four-family flat with four rooms on the second floor. I liked it because it was close to my school, and it was only one block from the dime store where Obine worked. As soon as we moved, Josie got sick. She was in and out of the hospital. I was twelve, and I would catch the bus every day to visit. Obine had to work. Josie had lupus. It didn't stop her. She went to Rock High School on Grand.

Josie had a friend, Lula Bardo, who was fine and fast. She was sixteen. When she stayed with us she would sleep with me. She finally got hot one night and made love to me. It was my first climax. No one ever knew, but she would tease me when no one was around. I was glad when she would come to our house. Then my cousin Larry Davis moved in with us. He just got out of the navy, and he helped care for us while Obine went to her second job at Hi Wills Tavern. When Luella came over for the weekend, she would give him some. That was the end of Luella and me.

Before he came to live with us, Larry fell in love with Josie's friend Emery Evans, but she moved to California. He would write her and tell her that he was going to California. He joined the navy and was stationed in California after boot camp. He got a pass for the weekend and went to see Emery. Her mother told him she had gotten married and moved. He had only joined to get to California. Larry lived with us for about a year, and I learned a lot from him.

CHAPTER 7

Larry's nickname was LC. He taught me how to cook and iron my clothes. He was always neat and clean-shaven. He was a ladies' man. Even though the list of ladies was too long to name, one was Norvell. Norvell lived with us because her mother put her out.

Larry worked for Famous-Barr downtown. He worked nights, so he got home before we left for school. One summer morning, I didn't leave the house, but Larry and Norvell didn't know. Norvell, a light-skinned woman with curly black hair, knew how to strut her stuff with her bowed legs.

As I hid in the front room, Larry came in. They got into the twin bed. The bed was making a creaking noise as they made love. I eventually was outside the bedroom door, so I could hear. When Larry got up off her, I opened the door, and then (I thought) it was my turn. Remember, I was only twelve with no sense, but I tried. Larry grabbed me and told me he would beat my ass. I hit him in the mouth and cracked his tooth. I was able to run out of the house and stay gone until Obine came home.

I guess that messed Larry's thinking up. He knew he couldn't tell because he would be kicked out of the house. The following week, he got caught stealing from Famous. He was sent to the workhouse. When he got out of jail, he met Jewel Sutton, got a job at General Motors, and started a family. My favorite cousin and I still talk about the old days.

When Larry left, my cousin Mary Ezell moved in with us. She came from Mississippi, where she lived with her strict grandfather, Oscar Lee Middlebrooks. He was the famous ass-kicking police detective. We called him Daddy Lee. As we were growing up in the city, everyone knew him and feared him. He didn't talk much and didn't allow standing on the corners. He lived on Evans Avenue, three blocks from us.

Mary, whom we called Esma, loved to cook and eat greens. Obine would always have a big Sunday dinner, where Lucille's father, Roosevelt Shelton, would always be with us. He treated Obine like his daughter and us like his children.

Josie

Roosevelt was a sharp dresser and had a new car. He worked downtown at a suit-manufacturing company. His side hustle was selling suits, pants, and cloths for dresses. He kept me in dress pants and suits. Roosevelt calls Esma, nicknamed Pete, because we were in hard times, and we ate what was served. Esma didn't live with us long because Obine introduced her to Joe Hurst. Joe was a tall, big man. He was so light-skinned he looked like a white man. He was an embalmer of the Green Funeral Home in East St. Louis, Illinois. He also worked at the post office long enough to retire. After a brief courtship, they got married, and Esma moved to the east side. I love her. Her personality never changed. Joe died, and she moved to Colorado and then moved back to Mississippi.

Now 4056 Evans had only Josie, Obine, and me. Roosevelt would come by every day to check on us because Josie was sick. That didn't stop her from having a lot of young men as friends. Here's the list:

- Clarence Harmon (became St. Louis chief of police)
- Norman James (Northwestern University dean)
- Jerry Jones (U.S. government)
- Ralph Washington (deceased)
- Paul Brown (St. Louis Fire Department)

During the summer Josie and Fellis would sit out on the steps. Fellis Foxwell lived upstairs next door. Fellis was an attractive girl, and LC tried his best to get her. Fellis was interested in an army sergeant who visited every other weekend. They would sit out on the steps for hours. Josie was always outside too. Josie met Andrew Bell through Fellis. When Fellis went off to college, Andrew continued visiting Josie. After a year, he proposed. He talked to Willie about his intentions, and Willie tried to discourage him because Josie was sick. He reassured Willie that he would take care of her. They got married and moved to Kentucky. Now there was only Obine and me living in the house.

Obine learned the tavern business from Hi Wills. She had a man, Hampton Russell, who had a business. I don't remember how Obine got fired from the dime store, but she tried to get the manager, Mr. Brown, beaten up. She never talked about the manager or the dime store again.

She wanted to move to the east side, and I didn't like it for my school years. I ended up living with Lottie and Yancy Martin, who lived on Aldine, two blocks from Visitation Catholic School. They were like my grandparents but were actually my cousins on my grandmother's side. This was when I realized what life was like and making decisions.

CHAPTER

When I moved in with Lottie, her husband was sick with cancer. He kept her busy during his illness. Even though Yancy would curse her and belittle her, Lottie took care of her husband. Since I attended catholic school and Lottie was a Baptist, she would always talk about the Catholics. She told me I could eat chicken on Fridays because it was a fowl, not meat. She didn't like the priests and nuns. She didn't understand confessing to a mere man. No matter what subject we discussed, she was always right. I guess that was her release from her husband.

Later, Yancy died. I learned a lot from Lottie—independence and cooking. She was a very good cook. She and Yancy were in the chicken business. When he got sick, she had to pay someone to deliver the eggs and chickens to her customers. By the time I learned the business, the supermarket could get chickens cheaper than Lottie. She eventually got a day job working for a family in Ladue. She also took in laundry to make ends meet. She was stingy. She had money and managed it well.

Her day job also meant she had to stay over with the kids. So I was at home by myself two days a week. I didn't mind that because it made me more independent. I got a job at West End Drug Store on Taylor and Easton, delivering prescriptions on my bicycle. I worked every day after school from 4:30 p.m. to 8:00 p.m., Fridays until 10:00 p.m., and Saturday until 10:00 p.m. My father moved to 4744 Cote Brillante, just three blocks from me. I would visit him often. Willie and Lottie were the only people I could talk to about things. Obine would call about once a week, and we would talk for ten minutes. Obine and Lottie didn't get along. Lottie didn't like the way her new man treated Willie. I really didn't understand the whole situation, but Lottie would make me know she didn't care for Russell. I would find out later from Willie what really happened.

So I'm acting grown—I had a job, a bike, money in my pocket, and control of the house. I got up at six every morning because Lottie got up at six. After fifty years of getting up for her chicken business, nothing had changed. She was a hell-raiser. As she chewed her tobacco, she would tell anyone off and didn't care if she hurt their feelings. I thought that tobacco and snuff were nasty, but that was her high. As I became an altar boy, Lottie still got up to fix my breakfast. I looked forward to her homemade buttermilk biscuits. I was drinking coffee at that age because she said that I wouldn't go to sleep in school.

Everything was going well until she moved in Bernice and her son, Johnny. Bernice had a job with a private family, where she stayed all week. Lottie quit her job and stayed home to take care of bad nine-year-old Johnny. He was spoiled rotten. Lottie had taken care of him when he was a baby. After a failed marriage, Bernice moved back with Lottie. I had to help with Johnny even though Lottie favored him over me. I made the adjustment and moved on with school, sports, and my friends in the neighborhood. One of my grade school friends was Eugene Taylor, "Bean," who lived on Cousin Alley. He would spend the night sometimes. James Smith and I would walk to school every day. He lived on Cora Avenue. Johnnie McGrew, "Moe," was a good basketball player. We all played for Visitation. Johnny Smith was our grade school coach. He had attended McBride High School. He was an inspiration because he still was a very good basketball player. We all wanted to be good ball players like John. He and Josie were in the same class at Visitation. I kept in touch with John.

Visitation had some characters and a host of big families in the parish. Most of the families had more than one child in school. The tuition was one dollar a week, and if not paid, Sister would send a note home to have the dollar the next day.

The families I remember were the Raymonds (Sylvester, Melvin "Head," Calvin, Louis, Louise, Sylvia), who lived on Fairfax in a two-family flat. This family was rough, with Louis being the worse of them. He caused me an eye injury by running me into a coat hanger at school. I had to go to the hospital. I planned to get him. He used to bully Bean. Eventually, Bean and I jumped him in the school yard after school. Later in life, I saw Louis with his face all scarred up from cuts. I was bigger than him, so finally I wasn't afraid. He said he was in a car accident, went through the windshield. As I walked away from this Frankenstein, I didn't feel sorry for him.

The Taylors (Nathaniel "Rallo," Richard, Eugene "Ben," Mary, and Rose) first lived on Cousin Alley on the second floor. Then they moved to a basement apartment on Newstead. All the Taylor boys were athletic. Nathaniel was a great football player for McBride High School. Later he was a TV star on *Sanford and Son* as Rallo. Eugene and I ran together. When they moved to the projects, I visited a few times. Eventually, they moved to California, where Nathaniel lived. I talk to Eugene once a month.

The Davises, Rufus Charlie and Hugh. Hugh was always into it with the Raymonds or the Dennises. Hugh could fight. He and Lorenzo had a terrible fight after school, and Hugh got the best of Lorenzo. They became friends after that fight.

One day, James Smith took his father's watch to school without permission. Before recess, he took the watch off and placed it on the windowsill with his sweater. He was so busy playing basketball he forgot about the watch. Hugh stole the watch. James was too scared to tell Mr. Marshbanks who took the watch. He knew he was no match for Hugh. James learned two lessons from that, and so did I.

The McGrews—Mach, Tallo, Bowgigle "Moe," Johnny, and Annie. Moe was my friend. He got me in with the gang. He was a year ahead of me. He worked with his father, washing cars on Saturday and cutting grass for white folks in the county. They lived on Aldine and Newstead down the street from the Taylors. Moe taught me the ropes in the street about drinking wine, parties on the weekends, and girls.

Moe kept money. After Moe graduated from Summer, he went to the service. I went to college. Later, I saw Johnny McGrew by mistake while I was looking for my father. Johnny was very sick with cancer. He died before I could go back to see him. I remember how we used to drink J. W. Dant whiskey. I couldn't drink much because Lottie would smell it on me. We could go anywhere to party, because Moe had a gun. We also would go to Danceland, where the other fellows were going.

I graduated from Visitation and started attending Blessed Sacrament Junior High School. I would have had to walk a mile and a half to school, but James Smith's mother took us. Mrs. Marshbanks was an attractive woman who worked as a nurse at Homer G. Phillips Hospital. Mr. Ishmal Marshbanks, "Ish," was mean.

The new school was different because there were about four hundred students. I had to adjust to the classes. The basketball coach told us we had to make at least a C grade to play. I loved the game, and I made my grades. I wanted to be a good player like John Smith.

That year was fun. The kids would misbehave in Mr. Richard Wheley's class because he couldn't see very well. Earl Harvey would always have the class laughing to the point of getting out of control. That would be when Mr. Wheley would hit the desk with a large yardstick. One time, he missed the desk and hit himself. We rolled.

I can remember my first freshmen basketball game. I hit fifteen that day. My father and uncle Daniel came. I knew I had to play well. We won, and I thought I was on my way to being a pro.

My first girlfriend, Anita Black, lived down the street on Aldine. She had a brother named Bubba. Anita was cute. She went to Sumner, and I would go to her house when her mother, Mama Mae, was home. Anita loved to kiss, but that was all. Never could take it to the next level. I did enjoy her company and being able to go to her house. I was just a freshman. Forty years later, I saw her at a funeral. She still looked good, just aged. We exchanged numbers for an upcoming golf tournament she was sponsoring.

Around the corner from my house was where my real first girl-friend lived. Barbara Porter. She was built and as black as night. She had a bright smile, but she was shy. Her mother, Mrs. Green, had two sons. I would stop by her house on the way home. She would come downstairs, and we would kiss in the hallway. She taught me how to kiss—the real deal. We made love. One day, she stayed home from school, and no one was home. That was the beginning of me thinking I could talk women into being with me. I thought it was the conversation. Barbara and I were friends until she died. I will always have pleasant memories of her. The last good conversation I had with her was when I was in my freshman year at Missouri University, Columbia. During a trip home, she told me she was marrying Johnny Parish, who lived on Garfield. I was hurt and tried to talk her out of it but to no avail. That marriage didn't last long.

After the failed marriage, I was home from school for summer. Willie and Emma went to Tennessee and asked for me to check on the house. I called her, and we met. We made love that afternoon. I walked her home. Years later, I talked to her cousin, who told me that her son looks just like me. To this day, I don't know for sure.

CHAPTER 9

The years at De Andreis High were the time I began the molding process. I tried to make a name for myself. I wanted to be a good student and athlete. I was going to a catholic high school, and all my friends went to Sumner. I met a lot of new people catching the Taylor bus to school.

July 15, I was a sophomore, and I joined my first football team. My coaches were Al Andrewlege, Jessie Horstman, and Kim Tucci. Today, Kim Tucci owns the Pasta House Company. Jessie Horstman died some years ago.

James Smith and I were still partners. I played football for three years. We did everything together. James, "Smitty," was a tackle, and he could hit. We had a good team. You would have to maintain your grade point to play for DA. John Warren and I became good friends. He was a right end and I was the left. John was also a track man; he was fast. Both of us could catch the ball. I didn't like to get tackled. So when I would catch the ball, I would break down the sideline to get away or get out of bounds.

Mike Cordes was the quarterback. He could throw that football on the numbers. I ran my first touchdown against Western Military Academy at Warrenton Missouri for sixty-two yards. The next touchdown was at Mercy High School for forty-two yards. Our team was made up of fast running backs. Ellis McMurty from the huts made his name in the CAC Conference. He was fast and could make tackles miss. Ellis, John Warren, Jame Smith, and I were all very close friends. Ellis was kin to the Franklins. They lived in back of us in the huts. Ellis left DA and went to Beaumont High with thugs. We tried to talk him out of leaving, but he didn't like the head coach, Al. He didn't like anyone correcting him, especially if he hit the wrong way on a play. All that and he never played for Beaumont.

Vincent Wright was a big, strong, fast fullback. He made a name for himself at DA. After graduation, he joined the city fire department and was assigned to the Salvation Army to help families whose homes were burned out. He had a heart attack shoveling snow. He loved Alice. He was a good guy.

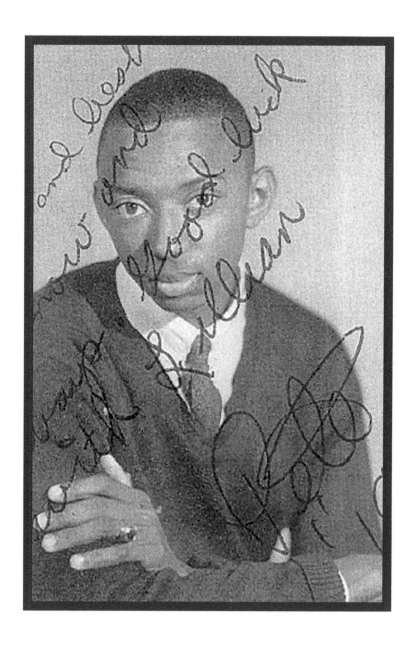

Homecoming

Neal Chastain, Maria Yim, Glen Flacke, Linda Kosarek, Frank Deutsch, Carolyn Westerheide, Judy Lerch, Queen Joyce Necker, Mike Cordes, Jim Smith, Linda Ross, Dan Schmatz, Mary Tomiser, Jim Jacks, Pat Rudloff, Crown Bearer-Joyce Necker's Nephew, Michael Thornton.

Dowell

Left to right, top to bottom, first row: Coach Horstman, Coach O'Keefe, Tom Farishos, Tom Wilmering, John O'Brien, Mike Price, Marty Dunne, John Cuneo, John Owens, John Koelker, Ken Hune, Coach Androlewicz. second row: Vincent Wright, Ron Weiss, Frank Bommarito, Don Cole, Darryl Jones, Hank Urbanowicz, Phil Locke, Gerald Tipton, Neal Chastain. third row: Bob Orzel, Ed Jones, Clem Sanders, Tom Burkhart, Gene La Valle, John Wiseman, Mike Marfori. fourth row: Ellis McMurtry, Patterson Spears, Jim Jacks, Frank Deautsch, Pete Smith, Dan Schmatz, Willie Dowell, Glen Flacke, Mike Cordes, John Warren.

John Warren, James Smith, and I were called the big three because we did everything together. John's cousin Marlene Hampton lived with John during the week. Since her family lived in Webster Groves, it was easier for her to stay in the city. She attended Harris Stowe Teacher's College. She was older than me, and she knew the ropes.

Marlene was off on Mondays. That was the day she would take her mother to work at the welfare office on Euclid. He father, Rich, was a lean, tough, fast-talking car salesman. She and I would talk on the phone at night. One night, she suggested I skip school one Monday. She would pick me up at the bus stop on Taylor.

That was a big house in Webster Groves. I was glad to play hooky. For one whole month, I did it and didn't go to school on Mondays. We had to be careful. I would get down in the car so no one could see me. John's dad, Alkins Warren, was stationed at the Eighth District Police Station on Deer Street. He really couldn't see me with her.

Marlene was short and built. I couldn't imagine what that first time would be like. Before we got to the house, she stopped at McDonald's on Manchester. I was still lying on the backseat. Because her grandmother lived down the street, I had to wait until she pulled into the garage to get up. I can still remember the automatic garage door opener, and finally, we were in the house. We ate the food, and she fixed drinks from her father's whiskey.

Her bedroom was on the third floor. Man, did I love how she made me feel. We would do it all day until 1:30 p.m. I fell in love with her. I was a fool each Monday. I finally got caught. Since I never skipped school before, I didn't know that they checked when you were out. Father Kirksey went to my house and told Lottie about my absent Mondays. The cat was out of the bag. Father contacted Willie on his job. So now everyone knew. To make matters worse, someone dropped a dime on me. They said they saw me getting into a car before school was out.

Father told Lottie the type of car I was in, and she knew it was Marlene. Lottie waited for me that Monday. She was nice to me when I came home. She told me to cut the grass while she fixed dinner. After dinner, I began washing dishes, listening to KATZ on the radio. All of a sudden, I felt a stick hit me across the shoulders. Lottie was standing there with her .45 automatic pistol and a cutoff broomstick, yelling and hitting me. "You bastard, skipping school with that bitch!" She caught me by surprise. I was scared she was going to shoot me. I booked and ran up to my father's house on Cote Brilliante. It was after four, and he was home. Emma was cooking. I told them that Lottie pulled a gun on me, and she had lost her mind. Willie was in his underwear, sipping White Horse scotch. As I showed him the bruise on my back, I was telling how she had hit me. He quietly asked if I had gone to school. I quickly said yes. He rose up out of his chair. "Since you lied to me, go in the bathroom and wait for me." He made me take off all my clothes as he told me that he knew about my Mondays with that girl. He locked the door so Emma couldn't stop him, and he beat my ass. He preached about lying every time he hit me.

After I put my clothes on, it was time for the lecture. He told me that Baby and Effie were in prison for lying and stealing. He didn't want me to grow up lying. I thought I was getting away from Lottie because she was the only one that knew. I jumped out of the skillet into the fire.

As I walked through the door at Lottie's, she laughed and told me she would shoot next time. I couldn't use the phone. I couldn't talk to Marlene. I went to the drugstore to call her, but I didn't tell her what happened. She tried to get me that next Monday, but I made up an excuse. After about three weeks, I called Marlene and told her I would visit her on Friday night. I caught the bus all the way to Webster Groves. I was hot, and I knew she was too. When Marlene opened the door just a little, she told me she had company. I could see the dude sitting in the chair. She closed the door, and I was mad. I later found out that her boyfriend, Robert, was home from the service.

Looking back, I remember her turning his picture down when we made love. I also remember hiding under the bed when her father came home. He asked about the smell, and she would say she was on her period. I thought it was love. That was a long bus ride. Never been there since.

Marlene eventually married Robert, and James Smith married Marlene's sister, Ricky James, and Ricky had one son and divorced James after he got out of the navy.

From left to right, bottom to top, first row: Coach Horstman, Bob Cole, Pete Smith, Bob Tracy, John Warren, Willie Dowell, John Wiseman. second row: Rav Behan, John Koelker.

10

BASKETBALL

Now we're in the basketball season at DA. The team was good. Before Amon Evans graduated, he broke Jodie Bailey's record for most points scored in a Christmas tournament at Ofellon Field House. Amon, "Horn," would shoot the jump shot and smile after he made it. Amon went to Rock Hurst College because of his good grades. He eventually settled in San Francisco with his family.

Years later on a trip to San Francisco, I saw him driving the Powell Street trolley. After work, he picked me up and took me to his home to meet his wife. We went out to the Filmore District and had a good time. I never saw him again. I was saddened when his sister, Emory, told me he had been killed in a motorcycle accident.

Now it's my senior year, and it's basketball time. I was on the first team with Bob Cole, Bob Tracy, Darryl Jones, and Soup. James Smith, John Warren, and Hank Oberinovietz all played. Ivan James was the manager. We were twenty-four and four overall with only four losses. The one loss I remember was against CBC. Bob Cole was a junior when we played CBC. Jessie Horstman, our coach, told us this was an important game because CBC had not lost a game. They came to our gym, which we called the snake pit because there was no room on the sidelines. The bleachers were close to the fault lines. Most teams didn't like to play at DA's gym. CBC had two guards, Kilo and Gunnerspot, we had played against in grade school. John Smith started for St. Louis University, and John Bennington was the coach at the university at that time. He was at that game, and there were many scouts from different colleges there also. I was proud that John Smith was there, because he called me Willie and sat in the stands with his coach. I was averaging about twelve points per game. Bob Cole was our gun, and he could jump over people. He didn't miss many shots, especially inside the paint. I started with John Warren, Bob Cole, Darryl Jones, and Bobracy. We played them and maintained the lead into the third quarter. I had hit eighteen points by the fourth quarter. CBC had double-teamed Bob Cole. They roughed him up and made him mad. Bob got into it with one of their players. He elbowed the player and got into foul trouble with four fouls. I took over the game and continued to score points. I had twenty-five points with eight minutes left in the final quarter. The coach called time-out, and we were leading CBC by six points.

Jessie told Hank to check in for me. When the time started, Jessie told Hank to give the ball to Bob Cole. CBC caught up to us, and the lead was two points. I was still on the bench with five minutes left. My father, Willie, and Mr. Warren were sitting together at that game. John Smith was sitting above our bench by the scorer's table. I looked at John, and he shook his head. I did not go back into the game. Cole couldn't score, and we lost the game by three points. After the game, Jessie talked with Bennington, and he came to the locker room. He said, "You don't have to be ashamed. You did your best." I lost my admiration for Jessie Horstman then. He threw that game, and everyone knew it. The deal was he wanted Cole to shine, but I was the star of that night. For some unknown reason, he sat me down.

DA was twenty-four and four seated four in the state regional at Hadley Tech. We won the first two games and would play Sumner the next game on Thursday night at seven o'clock. All that week when we rode the Taylor bus, the Sumner students would tell us we couldn't beat them. We wore purple jackets with white sleeves. You could see those letter jackets a mile away. We wore them because we were De Andreis, the Catholic basketball powerhouse. Amon Evans and Ernie Miller were responsible for its history.

The team had to get to the gym by themselves, and at that time, Hadley was in a tough neighborhood on Grand. Most of the students who attended Hadley lived in the projects. Hadley was playing after our game with Sumner. Everyone knew it would be Hadley or Sumner going to the state games in Jefferson City. The team waited in the hall for our coach. When he got there, we went to the locker room, and he was mad because, being white, he had trouble with some of the Sumner people on the parking lot. As a whole, the team had been talked about all week long. The students told us they were going to beat us down. This was when we showed the public schools we could play.

The game started, and I hit the first eight points on the board. Sumner was playing Bob Cole close, which left me and Darryl Jones open. We hit every shot. Every time Sumner got the ball, they tried to run and shoot. When we got the rebound, we would slow the tempo of the game down and work out plays and score. Sumner was used to running a team with fast breaks, but we slowed the ball down, overplayed each man on defense. They didn't know we played defense very well. We beat Sumner that night by ten points, and we all had to leave together from the gym. No Missouri state for them this year. I ended up with twenty-one points that night.

The next game, we played Hadley and lost by fifteen. James Gant did his job.

After the Hadley game, I met Eldridge Bryant and his girlfriend, Ethel Foster. I also met Ethel's sister, Lillian. My father let me have the car that night, so I took them home. The season was over, and I had made new friends. Eldridge and I started hanging out together because he lived on Garfield off Taylor. Bryant liked Lottie's cakes, and she like Bryant. He would come to our house, and I got to know his family and brothers. Bryant's dad had an old green car that would stop on us, and Bryant would restart it with gas he kept in a soda bottle. I started going with Lillian Foster during the summer. I was eighteen and was going to Missouri University in the fall. Bryant had a scholarship to Arkansas A&M University. That summer, we went to parties and dances. My dad, Willie, got me job at the packing-house where he worked. I had money every Friday. I would go down to see Lillian on Warne Avenue. I liked her because she was smart and said she wanted to be a doctor. We would play around but never anything. I didn't get inside her. Bryant was getting it from Ethel all the time. I made like I was doing the same with Lillian, but not like that.

If you noticed, I didn't talk much about Obine while in high school because she lived in East Boogie. I would go over there on the weekend to see her at the tavern. All my friends would go there because we could drink at eighteen across the pond.

CHAPTER *11*

MIDWAY MOTEL

I'm eighteen now, and I've really started being a man. Obine would have me catch a bus on Fridays after school to see about her and Russell's motel in Highland, Illinois. It would take about an hour from downtown St. Louis. Mr. Russell was leasing this motel, which had eight cabins on it. It was located about three miles from Highland on highway 55.

I would rent the cabin out and collect the money. I would clean the cabins even if they would stay for a short time. It was mostly a transient business. It was really dark at night, but as soon as I rented all the cabins, I would put the No Vacancy sign on and watch TV until I went to sleep. By daylight, Obine would show up and collect the money and say she would take me back to Lottie's house and give me twenty dollars. Obine said she had bills at the tavern to pay. From that time on while working at the Midway Motel, when someone would rent the room for only a few hours, I would clean it and rent it again. I would keep that money for myself. I would be smiling when Obine would give me that same old twenty dollars. I looked forward to going up there on the weekend. The rate for two beds was twenty-four dollars for the night. Remember, this was 1962. I had already applied to Missouri University and couldn't wait for school to start. I said farewell to Lillian Foster and left for MU.

James Smith and Robert Marley were my roommates at 104 Defoe Hall. When were checked in to the dorm, Robert was sitting on his bunk, reading a book. We introduced ourselves, and Robert told us about himself. Robert was about six feet five and skinny with a receding hairline. He wore thick glasses and had on house shoes. We unpacked and headed to the student union, where the young women were hanging out. When we got there, all the blacks were there dancing and drinking. This was a new life for me away from Lottie, Obine, and Willie. No one to report to and I could stay up all night long. I could drink and get with hot women. There were plenty of them. Every day for a week, we were at that union, partying. The next week, classes started, and it was time for study. I was in the school of education, and James was in arts and sciences. He wanted to be a doctor. Robert was in forestry. When he told us that was what he was studying, we laughed and so did he. He told us that he was twenty-five years old and a freshmen like us. Robert said he had been to every college in St. Louis, and if he didn't make it at MU, his parents were gonna stop his support. He admitted he had flunked, and forestry was the thing he figured he could pass to stay in school. He told us that we better stay away from that union, because the Greyhound bus would be carrying a lot of people home in January. Most students were there on academic probation, which meant if you didn't make a 2.0 grade point, you would be going home. Even he was on probation, and he had to make it. This was the first time I had heard this. I didn't know anything about probation, so I checked it out. I wasn't on probation, but James Smith was. I had a class on the far end of the campus at seven thirty, Monday, Wednesday, and Friday. I had sixteen hours of courses. After the first month, I adjusted, and I did listen to the Fez. We called Robert the Fez because he had a book in his hand every time you saw him. When he went to the toilet, he had a book, and he would warn us about getting in the library and studying. He told us to leave the women and Kappas alone because we'd be on the Greyhound. They would still be here. The Fez was so serious because he had to succeed. He had been like us. I believed him, and I started hanging with him. James Smith was in love with Judy Peese. He was on her, and he would say, "I'm gonna get that pussy from Judy."

The weekend was always the big thing. Either you went home or someone found somewhere to go, like over to Lincoln University in Jefferson City. The football game would be on Saturday, and we would go and, after that, party. We decided to help our grades by joining the Kappa Alpha Phi. It took time and money to be there, and I started out, but I quit because I didn't want to flunk out. I had a lot going on. I had a job in the mess hall so I could eat and pay my tuition. It was work study. Willie and Obine paid for my housing, which was only eight dollars a month. The only thing I had to do was make my grades.

The first semester was hard, but I got through it. I met Delores Miles at Missouri. She lived up the hill in the huts. She was a sophomore graduating from Hadley High School. She told me to pick my classes myself to build up my grade point. She told me that when she first started, the advisers would give the blacks too heavy a load. You would get a low grade and then get put out. She told me that she was good in French, and she was taking all French classes so she could stay at the university. Today Delores is a French teacher in St. Louis. She did make it. I saw her in 2007.

The midterm grades were posted; I didn't go to see mine. I waited for a letter that never came. I made Cs for the midterm. I began going home on the weekends to see Lillian Foster. I would stay at Lottie's, and on Sunday, I would go to Lillian's until it was time to go. Lillian and I would kiss, kiss, and kiss some more but never had intercourse. I would be dry grinding. Lillian was a good girl, and I liked her, but I put our education first. We talked about not screwing because she might get pregnant. We always talked about what we were going to do after we graduated from college. She was going to Harris-Stowe at the time. Lillian was very smart, and we had intelligent conversations all the time. Her intellect attracted me. While at school, I would talk to her for an hour on the pay phone. I would write letters and told her we would get married after college.

Meanwhile, I knew Molly Wittmore, who was a fine, built tall green-eyed sister at Missouri.

Molly was a sophomore, and she liked to talk with me. I kept her smiling and laughing when we would meet at the union. Most of the black students knew one another after a few weeks. I became friends with Johnny Roland, George Seals, and Carl Davis. They were football players at Missouri.

Johnny and George liked me because they said I was cool. George liked Gladys Pierce, who was a classmate from De Andreis. George said he wanted to meet her, so I set it up, and they started going together. Gladys was a friend of John Warren. She lived across the alley from John Warren in St. Louis.

When I got my first check at the university, I asked Molly out on a date. She said, "You don't have a car." I told her I could get one. She said, "Get the car and we can go to the Hink." I asked what that was, and she told me that it was where people went, parked, and made out. She insisted on me getting a car. I went back to the dorm and told the Fez. He told me that she was good at the game because she knew I was not going to get a car. I was a freshman, and she was a sophomore. So I probably wasn't the first. I had a hard-on for her. I could see myself being with his fine woman. The only one I knew that had a car was Johnny Rowland from Corpus Christie, Texas. I went and told Johnny I needed to borrow his car to take Molly to the Hink. George Seals's eyes bucked, and Johnny said, "You don't say." I told them that she suggested it. Johnny told me to get that pussy. I called her at the dorm and told her I would be ready Friday night. She agreed. We met at the union and left there and went to the Hink and made passionate love but no pussy. She said "Next time," because it was getting late and she had to be back before 1:00 a.m. I took her back. I took Johnny's keys to him and told them that she promised it the next time. Johnny told me I could get the car when she was ready. Everyone on campus knew about us. You knew I had to be about something if Johnny Roland let me have his car to get with Molly. I stuck my chest out and continued to press her. A few weeks later, Wanda Morganfield, who lived in Molly's dorm, told me that Molly's boyfriend had been coming up from St. Louis and getting Molly.

They would stay at the Columbia Holiday Inn for the weekend. I guess she told me that so I would look like a fool. I still was trying to talk to her. I didn't let her know I knew about her friend.

Everything was going well: grades good, got cash, would run home during the month to party. Eldridge Bryant would be home at the same time, and we would meet at Lillian's house on St. Louis Avenue and Vandeventer. We had fun, then I would go back to school to study. Bryant said he had to go home to see Jean and make love to her. He was in love. It was hard in Arkansas because the women were tight. They weren't giving up anything.

I had a lecture on Mondays, and Jerome and Jerad Hollins sat next to me during the semester. The twins lived on the other side of the campus. They had graduated from Sumner High and knew Lillian Foster. They told me they were going home because the Qs were having a dance. The following Monday at class, Jerad told me that the word was out that my girl Lillian was pregnant. I said, "What! No, that's not possible." I had not been home for more than six weeks. When I got out of class, I raced to the pay phone. She was not at home, and I called back late that night. I questioned her about what I had heard, and she said she wasn't pregnant. I told her Jerad told me, and she still said she wasn't. The Fez and James wanted to know what she said. I told the guys that it wasn't possible because we had never really fucked. The Fez said she should know. I didn't think about it anymore because I had enough to do to make my grades. Grades were all we talked about. We burned the midnight oil, studying late.

Even though we had been talking, Lillian called about coming to Missouri's homecoming weekend. She said she would make the reservations at the hotel and pay for it. This was two weeks away, and I had already made plans with Molly for that weekend. I had to tell Lillian that she couldn't come and that it wouldn't look good to her mother.

The semester was over. I passed, and James Smith's mother was coming to pick us up on Friday. We were all happy. James got a letter the next day telling him he had been expelled and to clear out of the dorm room. James get nervous because he thought he got a C in

French and Algebra. He was already on academic probation, and I remember he had started studying more in the last four weeks. When James left the room to call his mother, the Fez reminded me that this would happen. Robert said James would not be the only one. He said the Greyhound bus would be full after loading up a lot of blacks. The man didn't lie. They cleaned house: Bobby Valley, Ron McIntyre, Gladys Pierce, and Julius Kirksey.

James's mother knew he had been expelled. When she came, James little brother, Bruce, was in the car. It was cold and raining. James wanted to drive. He did fine until we got to Warrenton. I was in the backseat with Bruce. James was passing a truck on the left and clipped the side on the right front of the truck's cab. He snatched the steering wheel to the left and lost control. The car turned over two times, and we landed in the middle of the grass between the west land of Highway 70. The car landed upright. I hit my head on the rear window and broke the window. We were shaken up, but nothing serious. I called my father, and he came to get us.

When I got home next day, I went to Eldridge's house, and he was sad. He got hurt playing football and wasn't going back to school. We went down to Lillian's house. She was wearing a sack dress. She looked a little stout and had gained a few pounds in her face, but I didn't trip on that. I was glad to be home. We talked about school and how things were going to be when we finished college. The next day, I went to Gary with my relatives for a funeral. I only saw Lillian for a few hours before I had to go back to school.

When I returned to the dorm, it was like a vacant house. Rooms were open with no one in them. They cleaned house for real. When I went to the mess hall to eat, you could tell most of the black men were gone, but the black women were still there. The talk was that they were told. Robert and I had more room since James was gone. I really studied hard because I realized what the Fez had been trying to tell us. The rest of the second semester was fun. Carl Davis and I were good friends. He called me Dirty Di. He taught me how to play the conga drum. Carl was a tackle on the football team. We would go to the Hacienda Club and play the drums with a band on the weekend. I enjoyed that. Carl could really play the conga drum.

Carl went to Soldan High, and now he was sophomore. I have seen him once since that Mizzou days. Johnny Roland got suspended for a year for stealing hubcaps. He returned to Missouri and played in the Rose Bowl. Johnny Roland played for the St. Louis Cardinal Football team and married Barbara from St. Louis. George Seals played for the Chicago Bears, and Gus Otto played for Oakland Raider. I was there at Mizzou with them. Johnny called me Di Yawl, Mr. Cool. I've seen him about twice since.

The second semester was almost over, and I never did get Molly. It had been a year at Missouri University now and three weeks before school was out in May. In late April 1963, Lillian Foster called me on the office phone at the dorm office. She said that she was at the bus station in Columbia, and she wanted me to go to see her. I walked to the bus station, and she was there, sitting on a bench outside. At nine thirty in the morning, it was a nice day. I greeted her and asked why she was there. We walked down to the pub to eat. Lillian had on a bright-yellow muumuu dress. It looked like a yellow table cloth draped around her. I told her she had gotten fat. She only said that her mother cooked well and that she wanted to get away for a couple of days. We ate and then went to the movies to see *The Big Country* with Elizabeth Taylor and Rock Hudson. After the movie, I told her she would have to go home and that she couldn't spend the night here. She told me that she had a room at the hotel not too far from the bus station. I took her to the bus station, and I went back to the dorm. Now I was troubled. I couldn't tell if she was pregnant or I was just dumb about something like this. She was tied down, and her stomach didn't look like she was pregnant. I didn't lose any sleep on it. I would be home in three weeks.

12

The weeks went by fast. Willie came and picked me up. I returned to Lottie's house; she was glad to see me. While I was at school, Johnny McClough had gotten married to Lorraine Brown. She had a daughter named Pamela. Johnny eventually left Lorraine, and she was back with her parents with another child on the way. They worked it out later.

I was home and glad to be away from the books for a while. The next day, I went back to the packinghouse and started to work for the summer. I called Lillian and talked to her to see if she was pregnant. She said no. I had no car because Willie gave my brother Willie B the car I used to drive. I walked or got a cab. Eldridge Bryant was home, and we would go down to Lillian's and stay for a few hours and then go to a party or the tavern. We weren't old enough but would get in and drink. We went to the Tropotan or Sorrento's.

I worked about three weeks before I got my first check. The money was good. I only had to give Lottie twenty dollars a week, and I would buy clothes at Wolff's Clothing, where Warren Davis and Jerry Harper worked. I went to that store every Saturday to buy shoes or jerseys. Everyone wore Bannisters or Chuches shoes. I was making over two hundred dollars a week. I would have to report to work at four in the morning. I got off at noon. I worked in the lard room, where I cooked all the fat in big pressure tanks. I didn't work hard, but it was a dangerous job.

One Friday in July, Willie went to Tennessee and asked me to watch the house. When I got home from school, I saw Barbara Porter, and she told me that she and Johnny had divorced. I called her and asked her to go to my dad's house to check. We checked the house out and checked each other out. We made love on Cote Brilliante. Barbara eventually moved out of the hood, and I didn't see her again for twenty years. The next news about her was her death.

I kept busy because the schedule was hard. I had to get my rest in the afternoon after I got off work. I usually went home and slept until 6:00 p.m. On black Friday, I got a phone call at work. It was Lottie, and she told me that Lillian's mother wanted me to go to their house after work.

I got off and took a cab to Lillian's house. I rang the doorbell, and Mrs. Foster answered the door in a sweat and ran upstairs. I walked up the steps to see Lillian and Mrs. Foster in the bathroom. Lillian was sitting on the toilet. She stood up and grabbed me for support. Mrs. Foster said "It's a baby" as she pulled the baby from Lillian's womb. The baby was out, crying, and I was in shock. Lillian sat back on the toilet. By that time, the police and medical team were in the bathroom with us. They told me to go out, and I did. Mrs. Foster had the baby wrapped in a bath towel, and the police told her he would take them to the hospital. I was standing there, looking dumb and numb and my heart beating fast. They put Lillian on a stretcher and put her in the ambulance. The police told me to get in with Lillian.

Lillian just lay there and didn't say a word. Her eyes were closed. I leaned over to her and told her that she lied and this wasn't right. She had tricked me. Now we were at Homer Phillips Hospital in the waiting room. The head nurse came in and asked for Mrs. Foster. The nurse asked many questions about Lillian. She asked who the father was, and Mrs. Foster pointed to me. I went crazy then, saying that the baby wasn't mine. She wrote my name down. I took the clipboard from her and tore up the paper. The police came back with the nurse. He told me to shut up and sit down or I was going to jail. I told him that I was being set up because that baby wasn't mine. He told me to wait until the nurse came back. The nurse told me Lillian said that William E. Dowell was the father. "That's you." It was on the birth record. I told Mrs. Foster that Lillian was lying, and I was mad. I left the hospital and had a long walk home. My pants still had the baby's blood on them. I was still in shock, and I saw my future plans for education diminish. I couldn't think straight. How could she do me this way?

When I got home, Lottie was waiting on me. You can imagine how I was looking. It was about five in the evening. Lottie commented, "She done had your baby." I turned to her. "She had a baby, but it ain't mine." Lottie said, "Stop your lies. It's yours. Every time you come home, you be at her house all night. Yes, young man, it's yours." I went upstairs to get out of those bloody clothes and took a long, hot bath. I didn't go back downstairs. I couldn't eat. I was hurt, and now I had to put up with Lottie and her remarks. She stayed on me about the child. I went to work and back home. I didn't go out. I knew by now everyone knew what had happened, but who would believe me? Lottie told me that she had been talking to Mrs. Foster while I was in school. Lillian had been to Lottie's about two times while I called myself dating her.

I was unaware that the women had been talking. Lottie told me that the girl didn't have a father and I should do the right thing and marry her. I knew Lottie was not gonna let this rest. I told her it was my business and I would take care of it my way. Three days had passed, and Lillian was not at home with the child yet. I went to the store, bought clothes and diapers, and went by the house. Mrs. Foster wasn't at home. Lillian's sister, Doris, let me in. Doris was twelve. She took the clothes and began to talk. She told me that I was nice and not cheap like Lillian's other boyfriend, James Dyson. Reverend Dyson's son, where Lillian went to church. Doris informed me that when Mrs. Foster would go to work at night, James would pick up Lillian. Sometimes she was gone until morning. Doris said James was teaching Lillian to drive. I asked Doris how long they had been seeing each other. She told me it had been a long time. "But James can't come anymore because Mama ran him off with a butcher knife about two months ago." Doris didn't miss much. I put it together. I was the fall guy. What would I do now?

Lillian was home the next day. I called and told her I would be by on Friday after work. I took my .32-caliber pistol with me to work that day. I decided to get the truth from Lillian. I got there about 1:00 p.m. Lillian was home alone. She let me in and got back into the bed with Renee. I picked up the baby and kissed her. I said, "Dowells look like Dowells, and she don't look like me." Lillian didn't say anything. I told her that I knew about James. I told her that if she lied to me again, I would shoot her because she had destroyed my reputation. Lillian said she knew it was wrong, but she didn't tell her mother until her seventh month. She told me that I would not have to support the child. I told her I was upset about the birth certificate with my name as the father. She said she would change all that and take my name off. I really calmed down when she said that. James didn't want to admit it was his child, and her mother had run him away. Lillian said they had an agreement. She apologized.

I told her that was good enough. I told her not to ever speak to me again. If she saw me, she should walk the other way. I left her and went home and never returned to that address. I did tell Lillian that she owed me something I never really got, and one day, I would ask for it to make up for this problem that was not going away. I told her I was hurt.

CHAPTER 13

The weeks went by slowly, and I didn't go out much because I was embarrassed and went into depression. Lottie had a daughter, Delmar Raspberry, whom I called Aunt Delmar. She would go into rages about anything. Her husband, Harvey, would give me little jobs like cutting his grass and painting. I did those jobs during my stay at Lottie's house. Harvey would buy me nice clothes. He was like a father figure. He lived two doors from my father, Willie, on Cote Brilliante.

The Raspberrys didn't have any children. Uncle Harvey kept money in my pocket by teaching me how to work. I thank him for that today. Delmar didn't work. She stayed at home and loved to play cards. Harvey worked for the Jost's Pipe Shop downtown on Sixth Street. Harvey was the manager. He had worked for many years under Mrs. Jost. The shop made handmade pipes and did repairs. Delmar and Harvey never got along. She would curse, and he would just shake his head, continuing whatever he was doing. Delmar would go off anywhere. She didn't care who was in their presence. I didn't know why she was like that until Lottie told me. Lottie told me that Delmar used to do day work at the Jost's home when she was a young woman after Mr. Jost died. Mrs. Jost and Harvey were about the same age. Harvey was a distinguished, handsome man with the gift of gab. He was a talker and salesman, and the white folks liked him. In her young days, Mrs. Jost was an attractive white woman with money. Harvey was her backbone in the business. When I used to work at the shop, I would always be cleaning. I was cleaning up in the basement, and Mrs. Jost came down to check on me. She had a stocky build, short hair, and was always smiling. I liked her. I visited the shop every time I was downtown. Harvey would treat me like a son.

Lottie said Delmar was cleaning up Mrs. Jost's bedroom. As she was changing the sheets, she found some of Harvey's gray-and-black hair in the bed. Delmar quit the job, and Harvey had caught hell ever since. Lottie was scared of Delmar. She wouldn't argue with her. Delmar was crazy. Lottie told Delmar what had happened concerning Lillian and the baby.

Delmar came to the house and got on me and told me I should marry Lillian. I told her that it wasn't my child. She cursed as she was trying to hit me. I told Delmar she was crazy. Then she went off. I hurried and left the house. Delmar didn't really want me there with Lottie because she thought Lottie would leave me some money at her death. Lottie told me the house was mine when she died. She had arranged that in her will with her attorney, Harwith. I really bought that hook, line, and sinker.

Delmar and Harvey owned property, and that was how she made her money. Delmar and Lottie put their money together without Harvey knowing about it. Lottie had cancer and had it since she was forty years old. She had both breasts removed during those years. Delmar figured she would outlive Lottie and get her money. They used to get into it about money because Lottie was giving it to Johnny. Johnny was no good to anyone. Delmar was right about him, and Johnny was stealing money from Lottie. He left his children for Lottie to raise. Lottie spent thousands of dollars to get him out of jail for beating up a fag teacher he was fucking. She raised him and treated him like a god since he was a baby. Johnny never had a job or finished school. The last incident was the rape of a white girl in East St. Louis, Illinois. Lottie paid and kept him from going to the pen. Johnny left, and now Lorraine was pregnant with Bow. Lottie took them in, and Lorraine did help by working at the post office. I left Lottie's house and moved to the east side with Obine.

HIGHLANDER BASKETBALL SCHEDULE

November 23—FPCC vs. St. Louis Christian		Home	8:15 P.M
December 6—FPCC vs. Meramec		Kirkwood	7:30 P.M
December 14—FPCC vs. Sanford-Brown		Home	8:15 P.M
December 17—FPCC vs. St. Louis Christian		Away	7:30 P.M
(Blair College)			
December 21—FPCC vs. FVCC		Home	8:15 P.M
December 23—FPCC vs. Hillsboro		Home	8:15 P.M
January 4—FPCC vs. Eden		Home	8:15 P.M
January 25—FPCC vs. Meramec		Home	8:15 P.M
January 27—FPCC vs. Normany	Normany Jr. High	8:00 P.M.
January 29—FPCC vs. Hillsboro	Hillsboro Herky Gym	8:00 P.M.
February 8—FPCC vs. Normany		Home	8:15 P.M
February 11—FPCC vs. Eden	Plymouth Jr. High	7:30 P.M.
February 18—FPCC vs. FVCC		McCleur	8:00 P.M.

The way it looked when Spectra went to press. Five of these twelve men will make up the first-string basketball team. At lower left, the five forwards are standing, and from left: McFadden, Willie Dowell, and Simpson; Kneeling, Gilbert Chandler, and Vic Scholar. At upper left are four guards, from left: Jerry Harges, Ronnie Ford, Leslie, and Eddie Cutter. Above at right are three centers, from left: Grady Thomas, Henderson Faulkner, and Don Denham

CHAPTER 14

The east side was a little cramped. Obine was glad to see me and opened the door to me. Mr. Russell was okay too. I made new friends, but I stayed in St. Louis most of the time. Obine helped me go through the process of getting a car. Since I was working at the packinghouse, I could pay for the car myself. I bought a red 1963 Impala convertible. I loved that car. I finally had something I was proud of.

I went to see Molly Whitmore to show her my new ride. We talked, and she told me she was going back to Missouri University at Kirksville. I told her I would go down there with her. She smiled as she told me she was going with Curtis, who played football down there. I tried to get her to go out, and she refused. I moved on.

I didn't have a girlfriend. Eldridge and I would go out on the weekend to parties. We would drink wine and try to date women.

I decided not to return to Missouri University. I was going to go to St. Louis Junior College at Roosevelt High School in the evening. This would be good for me so I could keep my job and get my education at the same time. The junior college was a good school, and everyone was going there. There were some fine women at that school. I used to take two or three of the women home after class.

One night, Eldridge and I went to a party on Highland Avenue and Kingshighway. Birlinda Davis was having a birthday party. Birlinda and I hit it off right away. I talked to Birlinda. I hit it off right away. I stayed until everyone had left, and I did get a kiss from her that night. I talked to Birlinda every day for two weeks. She invited me to her house in the 4000 block of Garfield Avenue one night. Her mother was nice to me and asked me some questions about my family, education, and what my major was in school. Mrs. Davis was a schoolteacher in East St. Louis. When she found out that I was in the Russell family and who Obine was, the green light was on for me. Birlinda and I started going together. She really dressed well because her mother believed in the expensive look. She dressed Birlinda, Delores, and Leonard Jr. well. When we went to a dance, Birlinda would always have a new outfit from head to toe. I belonged to the House of Lords Social Club, and we gave big dances.

Birlinda was very smart. She graduated from Southern Illinois in East St. Louis. Everything went fine with us, and during that time, I met Dory Bolden, Delores's man. Dory was known as a gangster, and he was from a large family that lived out on De Giverville Avenue. Dory didn't like Mr. and Mrs. Davis. Dory would rule Delores. He told me to watch out for Mrs. Davis because she would try to control what her daughter did all the time. Delores had a fast mouth and would get smart with people, like her mother. Dory warned me about her. I was in love with Birlinda, and I thought she felt the same. This time with a new woman, I started out having sex. Always using protection, we made love all the time. I asked her to marry me, and she said we could do it after she finished her student teaching.

Everything was fine until I bought her a ring and gave it to her. I moved from East Boogie to St. Louis and got an apartment close to Dory's house. He and I got real close. I was older than him, and we talked about our two women and the future. Dory would get information from Delores and tell me what was up with Mrs. Davis. Sometimes we would stay out real late, and Mrs. Davis would get on me about keeping her daughter out too late. She said it wasn't ladylike to do that. This was the beginning. When she got the ring, Mrs. Davis really began acting like she didn't want me around. We had been together for three years. Birlinda was my whole world, and everyone knew we would get married except for Mrs. Davis.

Birlinda called me and said she was coming to the apartment to talk. When she got there, she gave me the ring back and said we should wait. I said, "Keep the ring, and we will wait." Birlinda admitted that her mother wanted me to have it back. That didn't make me feel very good because I felt Birlinda could make her own decisions, not Mrs. Davis.

I called Dory and told him what had happened. Dory told me to tell that old bitch off. Since I worked at the packinghouse and went to the junior college, she thought that I was not good enough for Birlinda. All this time invested in Birlinda and the great times we had were coming to an end.

I took the ring back, and when I would call the house, Birlinda would not be at home. I went to the house, and she was not at home. Ms. Davis had control of the entire situation. So I went to J. C. Penney in Wellston, where Birlinda worked on the weekend. We talked. I told her I had been trying to get her. She told me she would go to my apartment after work around 9:00 p.m.

She did come, and we had a drink and talked about us. Finally we made love, and she took the ring back. She went back home, and I felt happy because I figured I had showed her he real meaning of our love. There was a dance that following Saturday, and we were going. She said she would get the tickets. The dance was in East Boogie. I had not been to her house since she took the ring back. I got sharp and cleaned my car up and went to pick her up.

CHAPTER 15

When I got to Birlinda's house, I noticed a new car in front with Illinois plates. I was sharp, dressed down, new everything. I was trying to impress all. They would compliment you when you looked good.

As Mrs. Davis opened the door, she said, "Come in, young man. Wait here just a minute." I saw another guy in the living room dressed up and sitting on the couch. Mrs. Davis came back, and she said, "Willie, let me introduce you to John, Dr. Johnson's son. He's going to be a doctor too. He's going to Washington University Medical School." I just stood there. He never got off the couch. Birlinda came into the room dressed up. I told her "Let's go," and she told me that she was going to the dance with John. Her mother was standing in the room when she said that. I didn't give them the satisfaction of my reaction. I just walked out the door and got into my car. I left and found my friend Flim Thomas.

Flim listened to me tell him what happened. Then we went out to Sorrento's for drinks and waited. I was going back to that house after midnight. While at Sorrento's, I talked to Norman James, who used to take my sister Josie out. I told him what happened. He told me that some love affairs go wrong. He said that if I tried to get her back and she didn't hear me, she didn't wasn't to be with me. He told me to face that and be a man about it. "Go and cry it out alone and get her out of your system." Me and Flim went back to Birlinda's and parked his car in the alley facing the house. We had a baseball bat and my .32 pistol. About 2:00 a.m., a car pulled up and parked away from the house with the lights out. Flim pulled up beside the car, and they were in it. I got out with the bat as Flim looked on. When

I went around to the driver's side, I heard Mrs. Davis say, "I wouldn't do that, Willie." As she was walking up, I could see the .45 in her hand. I got back in the car. "She crazy too." I went home and knew my chances of marrying her were gone.

Even though she wouldn't let me take her home, we met the next day at SIU to talk. Once again, my heart was beating for Birlinda. I couldn't wait to see her again. The next day, I went to SIU to find her. I looked in the cafeteria, and I walked around the halls. I saw a woman, Betty Fisher, at her locker, and she told me Birlinda went to an Omega function. I finally left for St. Louis. I saw Betty waiting for a bus to St. Louis. I offered her a ride, and she got in. She said she knew about me because her locker was next to Birlinda's. Betty was friends with Jackie, Paul's girlfriend. Paul was in our club. Betty gave me her number, and we talked on the phone a few times. Betty told me about Birlinda's new boyfriend, which I didn't want to hear. I think she was trying to see what I would say.

Things rocked on. As I was shopping downtown, I passed a marine recruiting office. I went in. Talking to the recruiter, he told me that they had a special program for college students. I didn't have to go into service for a full year if I signed that day. I would be finished with junior college, and I could sign up for warrant officers school. I signed up and felt good, not thinking about the war in Vietnam.

CHAPTER 16

Now in the summer of 1965, I got myself together. I was playing the field, and it had been four months since I saw Birlinda. I dated women from the college. At that time, I was playing basketball for the St. Louis Junior College. We won the Junior College Championship in 1965. The team consisted of James Buford, who later became president of the Urban League. Also on the team with me were Jerry "Hump," Harper, Ronnie Ford, Grady Thomas, Jerry Hayes, and Vic Shoulder, who works at the VA Medical Center now. We were all guns and could play. I would get good articles and pictures in the school newspaper about my basketball plays. I was unaware that Lillian Foster was the editor of the paper. I never saw her at the school and didn't know she left Harris-Stowe. I finally saw her in the hall one day and was not hostile to her. We talked. She kept writing good things about the team and me. I forgave Lillian, but I didn't tell her. I just treated her nice. There were many foxes at school, and one was Joyce Tankins. She was a fine woman, and I would take her home after school. Her mother liked me, especially when she found out I was the son of Sister Emma Dowell. Odell Douglas lived across the street on Wells from the Tankin resident.

Joyce was a nice woman. She was fine, had dark complexion with hairy legs. Her hair was always fixed, and she smelled good all the time. She was a virgin, and I was the one. She let me make love to her at my apartment once. After that, we remained friends. I was between Joyce and Betty Fisher. Betty was also a virgin, and again we made love at her house and my apartment. After Birlinda, I couldn't make up my mind.

One day at the packinghouse, I received a note to call Birlinda. I called, and she asked me to stop by after work. I asked if everyone was okay, and she just said to come by after work. Of course I agreed. When I got to the house, Mrs. Davis was speaking to me, asking about my family. Then she told Birlinda that she was going to the east side and she would be back late. The house was clear for us. She invited me in and said she wanted to make love. I stood up. I told her how I had tried to reach her even though she was dating other men. I told her what her mother had done, and Birlinda had turned her back on me. I walked out to my car. As I drove off slowly, I didn't let my feelings get me in her bed. I didn't call her again. I got Birlinda Davis out of my system so far as love was concerned.

I was dating Joyce and Betty. I loved each one because they weren't trying to get over on me. They treated me well. I respect Joyce today for her love way back. She still looks good and has that same beautiful smile.

While playing basketball for the college, I hurt my leg at work and took off sick for a week with pay. We had a big game with Missouri University that same week. I scored twenty-three points that night for the victory. When I returned to work, the personnel manager showed me a picture in the Globe-Democrat on the sports page. It was me shooting the ball against Missouri U. Mr. Bondy told me that my legs must have been okay and he laid me off for three weeks. Back then, three weeks' pay did me in because I hadn't saved any money. I moved back to East Boogie with Obine and still stayed in school. Obine was glad I was back because she wasn't making much money at the tavern. She had left Mr. Russell because of her boyfriend, Glenn Little. She thought Glenn was going to marry her. Mr. Russell and Obine eventually got back together when my brother Donald Russell ate some Drano.

Obine would come to the plant on Fridays to get my check to buy whiskey for the tavern. She always told me she would give it back on Sunday night. I would never get my whole amount of money. It would be about thirty dollars. I was staying there, so she figured I owed her my check. I didn't give her any mouth about it. She loved money and still does today. I did learn a lot from her when it came to business and money.

I liked the Silver Palm Tavern, especially the go-go girls, who would take off all their clothes and dance naked. My friends Ralph and Eldridge would get them and party. Sex with them was real common. It was something to do. Obine told us to leave her dancers alone because the dancers wanted to drink free. Topsy and Chicky were the main dancers, and they would shake that thang. They were loose. I was still dating Joyce and Betty.

I really started to enjoy my life now. I had a good job, a nice car, and two sexy women and the House of Lords Social club. Obine showed me the ropes about business. The first lesson was you don't mix business with sex; don't have relationships with your workers. Obine hired Marilyn as a barmaid. Marilyn was about six foot two, light complexioned, and had long legs and a big smile. This lady knew how to handle the men customers. Marilyn lived in the projects on the south side. I would take her home after the tavern closed each night. Marilyn knew that I liked her, but I wouldn't beg to get with her. After Marilyn had worked for about a month, she asked me to take her home. Sometimes Obine would take her home, or she would ride with someone else. I took her home, and she invited me to go up with her. She lived on the eighth floor. I had never walked her to her apartment. It was a small place but clean. She offered me a drink as she went back to check on her children and change her clothes. I could hear the shower running. I drank the gin and watched television. When she came back, she had on a long silk nightgown. I couldn't keep my eyes off the black mound between her legs. As she let out the rollaway bed in the living room, she said, "I'm the first up and the last to sleep." She seduced me, and it was good. It was so good that I would get her every time I took her home. Marilyn had me going until Obine found out. Obine cut her hours and let her work days so she would be gone when I got off work. It was good while it lasted. I had only seen her once since then. Obine told me that I messed up a good worker.

Third Battalion
Platoon 356

Commenced Training:
28 February 1966

Graduated:
25 April 1966

NOT PICTURED
Maj. H. H. Bair
Executive Officer

Lt. Col. P. H. Simpson
Battalion Commander

Capt. W. E. Means
C. O. Co. I

Sgt. Maj. R. C. Brown
Sergeant Major

1st Lt. R. L. Smalley
Series Commander

C/Sgt. D. T. Dye
Series Gunnery Sgt.

S/Sgt. R. C. Roper
Platoon Commander

Sgt. J. C. Harper
Sergeant Major

LC W. E. Dowell Jr.
Platoon Honor Man
and Blues Award

Sgt. D. Thomas
Drill Instructor

WILLIAM DOWELL

CHAPTER 17

Everything was fine until February 6, 1966. I had been with Betty fisher that night. There was a loud knock at the door at about 3:00 a.m. Obine got up and opened the door. I was in bed and could see these two tall white men in uniform. I thought it was the police. It was the United States Marines. They said that they had come to get Private William E. Dowell to go to San Diego, California, tomorrow. I got out of the bed, and they congratulated me and told me it was time to go. I informed them that I had a whole year before I was supposed to go active. They said that the marines needed me now. As I put on my clothes, he told me not to bring money, cigarettes, and no belt. It took about twenty minutes to collect me. It was cold as I got into a long green van with ten other men. We went to the Mart Building in St. Louis for medical exams and booking. After, we went to the airport and transferred into a truck to the airplane on the runway. When we got loaded, we took off to California. I didn't have time to call any of my women. It was like I had been kidnapped. I didn't know what I had done by joining the marine corps.

After the plane landed, a tall big marine shouted and told us to shut up. He told us there would be no talking from this point on. We walked to a courtyard and were instructed to stand on the yellow footprints and not to move or talk. We stood there for an hour before we heard a loud voice say, "Attention, I'm Staff Sergeant Roper, your platoon commander. I'm your mother, your girlfriend. I'm your everything. Your asses are mine. I got the job of making you a United States marine. Some of you maggots are not going to make it. I will only take the best men to be marines." They marched us to another building in a single line.

The marines were screaming at us and pushing us in line at the barbershop. Everyone was shaved clean—no hair. They made us take off all our clothes and put them in a box with our home address on it. We were all in a room naked in a single file. They made us get close to the ass of the next person in front of us. I could see a doctor up front. As we passed the first doctor, he shot me in the arm with a needle gun. They made us bend over and show our asshole. After that, they sprayed us under our arms, between the legs, and between the cheeks of our ass. Then we went to this big shower, and they gave us ten minutes to shower.

Still naked, now we were in the clothing line, where we received white boxer shorts. They threw the clothing at us to put in a green seabag. We put the clothes on, which were too big. The belt was too long, and nothing fit. The cap was so big it was on my nose. The boots were two sizes too large. We ended up on those same yellow footprints again. It was about 3:00 a.m., and you couldn't hear a sound. I hadn't had any sleep or food. They marched us to the huts, which were going to be my new home. Having been raised in a hut, I was used to a hut, but this was different. These marines were mean, tough, and they shouted all the time.

The sergeant told everyone to just take a bunk bed. He showed us how to make a bed with military creases. He told us we all had fifteen minutes to make the bed and stand by it when finished. Everyone was moving fast. Since I knew how to make the bed, I finished and stood by, while some privates were having trouble. Three marine crew came back this time. As the sergeant entered, everyone snapped to attention. Sergeant Roper walked past each of us and looked us in the eye. He went to the other side of the hut and stood in front of Private Huddleston. Roper grabbed the private and started choking him as he called him a conscientious objector. He pushed him to the concrete floor and slapped him on his bald head. The white boy turned red and started to cry. Roper said, "This piece of shit doesn't want to fight or fire a rifle. This is the worst kind of man living, not to want to kill the enemy. The Viet Cong will kill you, rape your mother and sister, and hang your little brother by his balls. You disgust me, and I'm going to make you wish you hadn't come out your mama's crouch." As the crew walked out and turned off the lights, they told us to get in the rack. I could hear Huddleston cry. It was real quiet.

As I dropped off to sleep, I began to think about home and my women. It seemed as though I had just gone to sleep when the lights came on and a trash can was kicked over. The platoon commander was screaming and pulling privates out of the rack. As he was kicking them, he was saying it was time to get out of the racks. They counted us and made us march in our underwear to the head (toilet). We were told we had ten minutes to shit, shower, and shave. After ten minutes, the commander would clear the head, and we lined up to go back to the hut. We made up our rack, dressed, and stood by it until they came back. Then we marched to the mess hall. Once everyone had their food on their tray, we would have to stand at the table before we sat down.

Final Inspection

W. M. Dowell

Once the sergeant said "Ready seat," everyone was supposed to hit the bench at the same time. We had to do that drill about fifteen times before we got it right. As soon as we sat and began to eat, the sergeant said, "Platoon 356." We would have to answer, "Platoon 356, I, I, sir." Then we were ordered to get on the road. I left the mess hall hungry. We went back to the billet hut to stand by for duty. Sergeant Roper assigned two privates to clean his quarters, whom he called house mouse. When he would say "House mouse," the entire platoon would shout out "House mouse, I, I, sir." This was a way of passing on a command to the rest of the platoon or a way of working as a team.

There was something to do every day, and it got harder. There were only three blacks and a few Mexicans in our platoon. I was the last man in the first squad. We marched, ran, and did PT. Boot camp was only eight weeks. Boot camp used to be thirteen weeks, but they cut it short so we could go to Vietnam. I ended up in the front of the squad. When we marched, Sergeant Roper would tell us to lean back and strut and pound those heels into the turf so they would know we were coming. He was talking about the other platoons, because we were in competition. Sergeant made me the platoon guide. That meant I had to learn all the pivot movements since they were counting on me. I was like the team leader for the entire platoon of men. Each week, we got better, especially at the parade field. I could march and use the guide pole.

We went to the final parade competition in our sixth week. You had to execute perfectly with your rifle and steps. After we left the parade field, the sergeant told us to put our covers (caps) on backward and told me to get to the rear of the last private. He began giving us marching cadence like it was our first week in the corps. I was puzzled, thinking we must have gotten a real low grade. This went on for about thirty minutes. Sergeant Roper said, "You are all girls. You can't march worth a dime. You're gonna pay. Get down and give me fifty push-ups." Everyone was down, and I was at the back while he was screaming at us.

As we approached the huts, he stopped the platoon and told me to go to the front. He told us to put our covers on right. We began to march back to our hut, and you could hear the boots hit the pavement all at the same time. We made all the people turn to look. Sergeant Roper said, "Guide, lean back and strut, I mean strut." And I really did as he said. When we got back to our billet hut, he told us to put up our rifles and gear and be on the street in ten at ease.

Graduation

W. M. Dowell

When he returned, he had a red guide ribbon, and that ribbon was first place. He said, "We won. It was a team effort. The smoking lamp is lit, and it's letter-writing time." The next three weeks consisted of the rifle range and the CMC run. You had to qualify with the rifle and make the commandant of the marine corps run before you could graduate. All the training as a recruit and a private was hard, and many didn't make it. I graduated as the platoon honor man. They gave me a new blue dress uniform and a two-year leatherneck magazine subscription. I was promoted to private first class with one stripe.

The next day, they gave me my classification as a 0311, which meant I was a ground trooper, a grunt, a killer. I had written Betty and Joyce during the eight weeks. I told Joyce I wanted to marry her before I went overseas. I would address the letter always with "Dearest Darling." I mailed the wrong letter to Betty. She got the marriage letter and had the wedding set when I went home. I returned home and got married to Betty Fisher in June 1966 at St. Engelbert Catholic Church on Shreve Avenue. The wedding night was spent in Alton, Illinois, in a small motel. Obine paid for the reception at the Carousel Motel on Kingshighway. We got gifts but no money.

I was home for only a week. I was going to Camp Pendleton for advance troop training ITR. The corps was getting me ready for the bush in Vietnam. The training was hard, with a lot of walking and playing war games. I looked forward to liberty call on the weekends. When I went to the corps in February, Ronald Jones was with me at the induction, and we met again at ITR training. Ronald and I went on liberty to Los Angeles for the weekend. Ronald had relatives there, and we stayed with them. It was my first time going to a pool party in LA. It cost five dollars to get in. We did have fun, but most of the women avoided us because they knew we were going to Vietnam soon.

The next two months went by fast. I was in the Staging Battalion. This was where you were stationed for overseas duty. The group of marines here were ready to leave at any time. The military police were assigned to the group. They would escort us to the mess hall and back to the barracks. The barracks were just racks without sheets. Two days passed before they gave us shots. The shots made me feel different. It's hard to describe, because I felt calm, like being drugged. Two days later, they told us to saddle up. The trucks came and loaded us up for the twenty minutes' ride to the airport. The seabags were dropped, and they ran us onto the commercial 707 jet. No one said where we were headed. The corps doesn't let you know things until you are there. I didn't care because I was physically tired, and I went to sleep. The airplane ran into a storm, and I woke up, asking the stewardess where we were going. She told me we would land in Hawaii for gas and then to Okinawa. I really felt good about going to Okinawa. I had heard about the island and the pretty women there. Ralph Harris, who worked with me at the packinghouse, was a grunt. He told me that the corps would make a man of me. He was my best man, and he was also in our club. I thought about him while flying.

I met Private Marshall while on the flight. We were assigned to the same barracks. We were stationed in Okinawa at Camp Butler. We went through mine and demolition school while there. After two weeks, they gave us liberty on the island. Liberty call was given about four o'clock, and we had to be back on base at twelve midnight. The town was crowded, and military men were everywhere. There were clubs and whorehouses everywhere. I got drunk and got a tattoo on my right arm: Marines First to Fight. I had Betty put in between the First to Fight. The experiences on that island I will always remember.

It was time again to get on the airplane, and this time we knew we were on our way to Vietnam. It would take us over eight hours flying time to get there. The captain told us we were making our approach to Da Nang, Vietnam. I looked out the window, and I could see firefights going on. You could see smoke with things blowing up on the ground. The plane landed safely, and both doors opened. We were told to get off in a hurry. As we got off the plane, you could see marines lying on the deck with their seabags. They were dirty, had torn jungle uniforms, unshaved, and looked mean. While standing in line, a marine lying on the ground said, "I'm going home to be with Jodie now. I've been here thirteen months, and you can take over now. Good luck. You will need it because you will be in the jungle tonight with the VC." We went to a staging area, where I got assigned to I Company Third Battalion First Marines. I was taken to the company office in Da Nang. I signed papers and was told to go draw my rifle from the armory. The marine told me to pick a rifle out of the box. The rifles were muddy, and some had blood on them. He said that they had just come in from an operation down in Chu Lai. I found one, and he told me to clean it. I got grenades and fighting equipment. I left the seabag back at the company area.

Two marines from I Company came to pick me up. It had gotten late in the evening, and they stopped at the regiment headquarters about twenty miles from Da Nang. It was dark now. Four other new marines and I were told to stay in the tent and lie on the floor. I had my rifle but no ammunition. I would get it from the company when I got out there. In the next thirty minutes, the VC began to attack the regiment. A sergeant told us to stay put. I was hugging the deck, and I could hear the bullets going through the tent. Everyone outside was running around and giving orders and firing. This lasted about twenty minutes. They called an all clear, and things went back to normal. I slept on the floor that night, hugging my rifle and thinking. Now the pace was too fast. I was in the middle of a real war, and this was very serious. The VC came to attack us. The sergeant said it happened all the time. The VC were close, and they tried to catch us off guard. He said that we got one tonight.

It was daylight now, and I felt better because I could see if something were to happen. A corporal came to take us to the company area. The truck drove for an hour deeper into the jungle. When we arrived at the area, I saw a bunch of marines living in foxholes on a hill and in the open like a filed. They took us to the platoon commander, who was Hawaiian and talked rough. He told me I would be in the first platoon with Lance Corporal Robinson. Robinson told me to put my gear by his and take a seat on the ground. He questioned me about where I was from and my background. He told me to stay with him and I would be okay. Robinson took me to talk to Sergeant Yarnell, who was the squad leader. He said that Yarnell didn't know what he was doing out on patrol. He went on to explain the daily procedure. We were to patrol the area for VC and go out at night to set up ambushes to try and catch them. The VC set mines and booby traps to kill us. It had gotten dark, and Sergeant Yarnell gave me more grenades and ammunition. He told me and another marine to guard some VC prisoners who were sitting in a crater on the ground. The air in Vietnam was foul, and it was hot in the day and muggy at night. The VC were tied up and not talking. I guarded them all night. I got sleepy.

CHAPTER 18

The Vietnamese captain talked to our marines, and they put the prisoners in the chopper and left. I saw death that day. I got relieved and went back to where Robinson was. He wasn't there, so I just lay down in the hole to sleep. Robinson came and said he had been on patrol. He complained again about Sergeant Yarnell. I couldn't do anything but listen. I went to sleep. I ate two boxes of sea rations, which is canned food. It tasted good. The next day, I just lay around all day and played cards and read books in the hot sun. I was in the same clothes I left the States in, and they had starch in them. The heat baked the starch into my skin, and I got a rash all over my body. Robinson told me to wash my uniforms and the starch out. He said, "No starch over here. This is the bush." Now I could understand why the marines at the airport looked like they did. I hadn't washed in three days. I watched Robinson and learned from him what to do and not to do. He told me not to volunteer for anything, stay out the way, and hide if I could. They would find some kind of shit to make you do. The next day, we were told to saddle up because the choppers were coming to get us.

Robinson told us to stay beside him because we were all getting some shit today. "This ain't good, man." The chopper came in a hurry. It was my first ride in one. Once we went in the air, it was hell. My head and stomach were together. I got dizzy because the chopper was taking deep drops and coming back up and down, rocking from side to side. Then I heard the guns on the ship firing and the smell of smoke. The chopper hit the ground real hard, and we ran out. I was on Robinson's heels, and we got down on the ground and began shooting our rifles. The choppers were gone, and we lay out in the field for a while, but the rifles were silent—no firing.

As we landed, Robinson told us we were a blocking force. I asked what that meant, and he said that the VC were going to be pushed to us because marines had gotten behind them. After two hours, nothing happened—no VC, no firing. We were told to saddle up. We were moving out. I could count about fifty marines in our group. Robinson said we were walking back, patrolling for VC. We got back to the company area later that day. We stopped about three times going back. I was tired and needed food. We ate and got back in the foxhole to sleep. After getting used to sleeping in a rack for months, the hole was home, comfort, and protection.

LCpl. Curtis Robinson taught me the ropes of survival

Robinson was the most important person in the world to me. He showed me the ropes and tried to teach me pinnacle. I began to read everything I could to pass the time and not think about home. I wrote to my wife. I looked forward to her letters. It was something to live for.

It was August 1966, and it was hot. We were told that we would move to another location in a few days. Robinson said it was a better place because it had bunkers already built in a little village down by the An Trach River. We went by truck to the village. There was activity with houses, a market, and a CP area for the brass. We were assigned bunkers that surrounded the entire village almost like a city block on all sides. The first few days were okay. We had a weapon and motor platoon and eighty-one guns there. I felt better because we had about a hundred marines. I got to meet all the black marines. We had an old brick building for a mess hall. I got in with the cook and told him I could cook. I told him I would help him if he needed it.

The next day, I got moved to bunker number 1 with another younger marine. His name was Robinson too. He was from Detroit. Bunker number 1 was sitting away from everyone else. It was almost like an outpost. It was a listening position hid under the vegetation of the jungle. It was very spooky and black dark at night. Robinson was not as cool as the other Robinson. I could tell he was nervous. He had two boxes of grenades, and he told me to throw one every fifteen minutes while I was on watch. We were the only two in that bunker all night. I kept my eyes open. I couldn't sleep because he was throwing grenades in all directions, saying, "You won't get us down here. I got something for your asses." I was in that bunker with him for two nights.

I stood guard on each bunker on the left side of the village that month. I knew all the grunts after about a week. My squad leader was Kerrens. He took me on patrol and made me walk the point. That was the place to get killed first. New marines always got the point on patrol because they really didn't know the other marines that well. So if they got killed, the others wouldn't feel attached to him. I walked the point and had a pump shotgun. I was very careful, and I remembered how I was trained back in the ITR. It was like hunting rabbits. You had to see in front of you on both sides and anything on the ground that wasn't natural. Each time we went on patrol, I was either at point or at the rear. We searched the area around Antrack twice a day and set up ambushes at night.

New marines joined us, and the old ones left to go back to the USA. When a marine got short, he wouldn't go out on patrol because he only had weeks before going home. They respected that because when someone so short went out, they would always get killed or wounded. Some would still go out anyway. Each squad leader tried to make a name for himself by trying to engage the VC and hunt them. Sometimes two squads would go on patrol together. This one sergeant would always take us down to the river. Every time he did that, someone got shot. He would call in the heavy chopper and phantom jets to bomb where the fire was coming from. The fire was on the other side of the river. This sergeant always went down there. One particular day, we got ambushed. The fire was so bad I moved in the foliage as a sniper tried to hit me. The bullets were hitting along me where I was lying. It got so close I rolled over in a small creek and fell in it. The VC could see me, so I had to move. The grenade-throwing Robinson was in front of me. I told him to get in the creek. I moved up to where he was, but I was under cover. He was still on the bank, and as he moved, I heard a smack-like sound. Robinson hollered and screamed in pain. He was shot in the leg. He started shaking and rolling. I grabbed him and pulled and got on top of him so he wouldn't get hit again. I told him to stop moving so I could hit him with the morphine. I called the medic. When the doctor got there, he worked on his leg as the sergeant called for a med evacuation. We ran out of there, carrying Robinson to the chopper. Robinson said "Thanks," and I told him he didn't have to worry because he was going home with a Purple Heart. That wouldn't be the last time to that river. It was the hot spot. Sergeant Price liked to go down and fuck with the VC. The marines were mad at Price because of his patrols. Between Price and Yarnell, the troops didn't like either of them but had to obey orders. I was new, and I tried to learn real quick what not to do. The marines who were short would always advise you. Every morning that chow was served, this one marine would always take a shortcut from his bunker to the mess hall. He would go outside the perimeter, open a small gate, and go to the mess hall. He had been warned by Robinson not to do that, and he told Robinson to get fucked. The following morning, that same marine continued his pattern. We watched as he opened the gate. As he entered the gate, the explosion went off by his right hand. The gate had been booby-trapped. The marine's hand was in shreds as he screamed in pain. We went to him very cautiously. Robinson told me to get down because we might be set up for an ambush. Robinson crawled under the gate without moving anything. Doc shot him up and called for med evac. Robinson told us that the marine could have been killed or got everyone blown up because the bunker was close to the wire fence surrounding the compound. After those three months, I had been through everything a grunt could experience except death. Someone would get hit or killed every day.

Sergeant Price took us to the river again. On the way back, Corporal Airs stepped on a booby trap that was on the side of the trail. Airs's right foot went down on a steel-pointed arrowhead that was attached to a large concrete block buried two feet in the earth. When Airs went down, he yelled in pain. Price then ordered us to get back and set up a 360 around the area. We had to be careful. The VC knew where we were. Doc hit Airs with the morphine and just laid him back on the ground with his leg in that hole. We had to call the engineers for help because we couldn't get that large block out of the ground. The med evacuation brought a hacksaw, and the steel rod was sawed off. When the chopper took off with Airs, the VC started shooting at the helicopter. Price was mad, and he ordered us to leave the area. When we got back to the platoon area, Price said that we would be ambushing them tonight. I knew we would be down by the river that night in the dark.

We left the area before dark. We moved and stopped about five times. I could hear the water as we approached the river. We set up the ambush and waited. It was quiet, and we didn't move. We sat there for three hours. We moved again and set up along a trail. Nothing happened that night. I admit I was scared, but I trusted Price. He had been in the country for fourteen months. He liked to fight, and he extended his rotation date. The marines knew he knew his way around the jungle and how to get to the VC. The VC had a price on his head because most of the chiefs of the villages knew Price. They knew he would kill and destroy a village.

The following week, Price left our platoon and went to recon platoon. We got Sergeant William Powell from Kansas City, Missouri, as our new team leader. Powell was tall, slender, and cool. He talked very slow and carried an M79 grenade launcher and .45 pistol. Powell told us he had been there nine months.

19

Powell's first patrol was not to be forgotten. Powell walked the point about twenty yards ahead of the fire team patrol. We went into a small village about three miles out from the platoon area. We had to do these patrols to protect the Vietnamese people from VC aggression. Some of the people would bow and speak to you in the day, but at night, some would be your enemy. When we got ready to leave that village, we got sniper fire from the rear of the village. Powell told us to get in a 180-degree perimeter. He approached the front line, telling us to spread out. The sniper fire increased. Powell started shooting his M79, and he could saturate an area with it. He walked from right to left, shooting and telling us to hold our fire until someone ran out of the village or at the tree line. Powell was shooting up high in the trees and walking the grenades back and forth. The snipers stopped, and no one ran out. If any VC were there, they went into a tunnel and got out. We got up and went back to the village, and Powell showed his leadership. He asked for the village head honcho. The old man came out. Powell asked him if he was the VC that shot at us. The old man just bowed and put his hands in a praying position, saying he didn't know. We searched the place and harassed the people. There were many women and small babies but few men. Most of the men were very old men, and they just bowed and put their hands in a praying position, saying they didn't know. We searched the place and harassed the people. The young men were driving troops or VC. We didn't find anything, so we left. I knew Powell could handle anything. We became good friends and talked a lot about home and what was going to happen when we got back.

I felt safe with Powell whenever we went out on night patrol. Powell would take us out in the front of the perimeter and patrol around the perimeter. He would take us back inside of the perimeter to Papa Son's house, and we would do our radio checks. We would stay in the village the rest of the night. Powell told us there was no need to go out in Charlie's space when you didn't know where he was. It was his jungle. He controlled it, not us. He said he was trying to stay alive, not be a hero.

Powell knew the way to handle the marines and what to do in any situation. We got new marines to the platoon each week. New marines got the hardest jobs, so it meant less work for us. The village we occupied was about twenty miles from Da Nang. It was called Antrack Village. It was in the south with not a lot of hard-core VC. But we did have snipers and a lot of harassing gunfire daily. I would write home often and look for letters from Betty. She did a good job writing, and I appreciated the tapes and letters.

I tried not to think about home too much. After four months there, I appreciated life now. It was minute by minute because any-time, you could get killed. Being scared was okay. You would have your times to laugh, sleep, eat, and be afraid of being killed by the enemy. I would read anything I could get my hands on because it took me out of Vietnam.

CHAPTER 20

We are in the monsoon season now, and it rained a lot. The rain worked to the VC's advantage. We stayed close to the village and ran patrols and tried to stay dry and warm. Powell and I spent a lot of time together. They would call Powell, and sometimes I would answer because they used the last name. With my name being Dowell we had that in common. Powell and I wrote letters to President Johnson, telling him how we were sitting ducks for the VC. We also said that if we shot someone who wasn't a VC, it was a mess. The mess got worse when we got a new second lieutenant as our commander. I can't remember his name because I didn't like him. One night, he tried to sneak up on me at my post to see if I was asleep. I shot at him. I had hell behind that shooting inside the perimeter. I got reprimanded. I was always on guard even when I was not on guard. Each marine took watch hour at night, in the daytime, in your hole, or in the bunker.

Every time a new officer of NCO came to the I Company platoon, they had to try and make a name or impression on the troops. The first day out with the new Louie, he called in an air strike on a village where we got fire. We went on hunts for the VC, and the new Louie had us jumping. Sergeant Powell didn't care for the new Louie either, but we had to follow orders. He would send out six marines instead of twelve. We patrolled at the same time instead of just one group out. We headed out and stopped in a cemetery to rest.

Private Culp was standing the door of a pagoda when Robinson told him to get down. As soon as Culp moved, a sniper put a shot into the pagoda. I ducked out the front and saw the jungle elephant grass move. I followed the movement because I was above the grass field. I ran and cut him off by shooting my M14 and spraying the area. I could hear shooting to my left, and I thought the squad was after the same VC I was trailing. I stopped shooting and walked very carefully until I saw a blood trail on the grass and the ground.

The VC was hit and losing blood, but I couldn't see him. I had gotten overcome by the shooting and remembered I was tracking the VC by myself, and there was only six of us out there. I finally heard the wounded VC trying to crawl. I found him. His legs looked like hamburger meat. I had shot him in both legs. He lay facedown when I approached, moaning in pain. I called out for the medic, and the rest of the team came with the doc. The doc told us to get back. He shot the VC in the head and tied a rope around his hand. He told everyone to take cover because the dead VC had a grenade under his body. When Doc pulled the rope, the body rolled over, and the grenade went off. We called it in to the platoon that I had killed a VC sniper. Doc gave me the VC's rifle and said it was mine. "Good job." The Vietnamese people came out and tied his body on a pole and took him back to the village to bury him with his face down. They said he was a disgrace to the South Vietnamese people. This shooting took place so quick. I reacted to the situation and killed the VC. I didn't feel too good about taking a life, being Catholic and all that stuff they told us in school.

The laws were different out there. It was kill or be killed. I learned that very fast the next day. The VC were mad because we killed one of theirs. We went back to that same area the next day and went into a small village to rest. We started out, and I had the rear guard. There were twelve of us that day. Sergeant Powell was on the point, walking slowly, looking. When the team got in the open, one shot was fired, and a marine was shot in the thigh rolling on the deck. When shot, the body reacts, and the shock takes over. That was why we had a navy corpsman with us all the time. The first thing the doc did was hit the wound with morphine and try to stop the bleeding. In a few minutes, the choppers were on the scene. A Huey and medivac chopper got the marine to the hospital in Da Nang.

We started to move out and went about one hundred yards, and another shot rang out. Another marine was shot in the back. A sniper was in the trees or in that village we just left. We went through the same ordeal again. Powell ran back to the marine and tried to figure out where the sniper was. Powell called back to the platoon and gave the grid coordinates. The helicopter came again, and this time, he took fire from the ridge. Another marine was shot when the chopper landed. They put him on the chopper because he was carrying the second wounded marine when he got hit. Powell got on the radio, calling for help. There was only seven of us now. He told us to run to the hedge grove of trees on the double. As we ran, the VC began shooting. We ran, got down, and got up and ran again. The VC fire got so bad we had to stay down on the deck. I looked around me, and there were grenades lying on the deck like someone had laid them there. I told Powell that this place was a trap. I got scared then because I figured a wire was set to spring an explosion. We made it to the tree line and set in a defense and called the company again. Powell said the second platoon was on its way. I was glad to see them when they got to us. Powell was cool. He told the platoon commander the sniper was in that village. He told us we were going back to the village. We did a frontal attack. The commander called in the gun ships to destroy the village. We watched the napalm drop from the fighter, and the village was gone. We didn't go into the village. We went back to the platoon area after setting out there for an hour, looking for any movement.

That was a terrible day. The VC got revenge. No one was killed, just wounded. Powell told me that was the tactic the VC used when they captured Americans. I was glad to get back to the platoon area. The other marines wanted to know what happened out there.

Gary Newton, St. Louis, Missouri

Came home and died in mower accident

CHAPTER 21

It kept raining for days. The river flooded, and Antrack Village was surrounded by water. The bridge to get to us was almost washed out. Sergeant Powell went to the PX. Coming back, they tried to cross the small bridge. The water washed the vehicle off the bridge into the flooded water, and Powell was swept under. As he was yelling for help, he was being washed toward down the river. One young Vietnamese boy got in the water and saved Powell's life. When the boy got to Powell, two more swimmers went to help.

When the water went down, I went to the PX in Da Nang with Gary Newton, my homeboy from St. Louis. He bought his girlfriend a ring, and we mailed it from the PX. Gary was happy about going home. It was now November, and I could start counting my time. I had nine more months of this place.

I asked to go to Da Nang when the next truck went off the compound. I didn't feel like carrying a rifle, so I took a .45 with me. I went to the PX, and another marine from the platoon told me he would go back with me after he made a stop. We went down a backstreet, and this marine was carrying a shotgun. There was a place that sold beer and soda. We stopped, and he talked to a Vietnamese woman who was flirting with him. He knew her because she dropped about ten joints of grass down the barrel of a shotgun. He paid her, and we left. We walked to the highway to get a ride a back.

I didn't smoke, but that day as we waited for a truck, I smoked a joint with my fellow marine. When the truck came, I was so high I could hardly get on the truck. It took about an hour to get back to the road that led to Antrack Village. We had to walk about a mile from the main highway. It was sundown and getting dark, and we were high and unconcerned. As we approached a bend in the road, a shot rang out toward us. We took cover and lay out on the deck to see what we could see. I sobered up real fast because I knew we would have to run the rest of the way to the platoon area. We started out walking fast as we looked ahead and behind us. I told the marine that it was time to run. We ran until we could see the lights of the village.

This would be my last trip to the PX with a .45 and one marine. We could have been captured, and no one would have known what happened to us. Getting high on a grass was common in the bush. Everyone smoked. That was my first and last smoke. Again I was glad to get back to my area.

The next day, everyone was put in the jungle as a blocking force for an operation. We were stretched out for about a mile, waiting for the VC. It rained all day. Because of the rain, we had no food. No choppers were in the air. Our platoon was near a small village, and no one was there but a large pig in a pen. I told the sergeant that I knew how to kill the pig and fix it. He agreed.

I had the pig dressed and laid out on green bamboo sticks over a fire with banana leaves covering him. Rice was boiling, and meat was smoking. Later that night, we ate pork and rice. I fed the marines that night. No enemy showed, and we hiked back to our area.

CHAPTER 22

When we got back to the platoon area, the Vietnamese people were cutting the foliage and weeds around all the bunkers in the village. They said since the water had gotten so high, it made the snakes think you were dead. They were small, less than ten inches long.

I was told to go to post number 10 and stand watch with Corporal Bishop. I went there at 0900, and as soon as I got there, we got incoming fire from the left side of the line. We returned fire, and this firefight lasted for an hour that morning. The sergeant checked the line to see if everyone was okay. Bishop told me he was going to go and get us more ammo and some sodas.

I was tired and needed sleep. Babyson came down to where I was and told me that Bishop was in the village, drinking. It was supposed to be three marines to each bunker, but Christensen had gone to R&R, and the two of us were to stand watch all night and day.

When Bishop showed up, he was high, and he lay down and fell asleep. I was mad, and I woke him up, and we began fighting. I got the best of him because he was drunk off rice wine and beer. He had been in the village fucking with the town whore, and he wasn't worth a shit. He knew I would have to stay up all night to stay alive, while he slept. I called for Powell to come over to our position, but he didn't come, so I was stuck with Bishop. Babyson stayed with us until it got dark, and I got few winks, while he watched out for anyone coming. The little boy washed clothes for me and ran errors for a fee. I told him all about America and said when I got ready to return home, I would take him with me. I really meant that, because I wrote Betty and told her about Tommy Mi, whom we called Babyson. Tommy would bring food that his mother cooked. The rice reminded me of shrimp fried rice back in St. Louis. Thoughts or little things like fried rice would take you back home to your neighborhood Chinese restaurant. Some egg foo young would be nice now. When reality came back to you, it gave you the will to live and to survive the war and get back to your loved ones.

CHAPTER 23

Earlier, before Bishop returned to the bunker, I talked with a new marine who just passed and started talking to me. He was black and from Philadelphia. We called everyone marine. He was with the weapon 81 group, which was in the middle of the village. His team had a tent and cots with nets over them. I told him to come and stay with me in the bunker and help me watch. I told him that the night guard watch would go by fast with three of us, and we could talk about the USA. He said no. He was going to get some sleep in his area. I thought it was a good idea. So I had to stay awake.

I had a radio, and it kept me company while on watch. Since the people had cleaned around the bunkers to keep the snakes away, the positions were more visible outside the perimeter. That meant that the VC could target the positions better with the foliage removed. The radio station gave the time of 0130, and the Supremes song "You Can't Hurry Love" started playing. Immediately I heard a dog bark behind me inside the perimeter. I removed the safety from my rifle and started to step toward the barking. It was dark, and I heard a mortar sound. The mortar hit the bamboo trees leaning over my bunker and exploded in the air. That mortar was meant to hit my post. The explosion woke up Bishop. I had started approaching my rear when I noticed two sets of eyes lying on the ground behind me. I aimed my rifle on them but didn't pull the trigger. I hesitated, and then a fuse-lighted grenade was tossed against the bunker and landed behind me. I knew what was happening now. The VC had me between them, and the grenade and I had to run and jump into the bunker. We were being attacked from the outside, and the VC were inside our wire behind each position we manned.

I ran and tried to dive into the bunker headfirst. As I dove, the grenade went off while I passed over it. The blast kicked me up about twenty feet in the air. I fell through the top of the bunker on the top of Bishop. I held on to my rifle through the blast. My shirt was in shreds, and my chest and lower body were burning like I were on fire. I couldn't see out of my left eye. It was closed completely. I told Bishop we had to get out of the bunker because the VCs were behind us. I told him to follow me.

I climbed out in front of my bunker and turned the claymore mine toward our perimeter and again told Bishop to get out of the bunker. I crawled into the rice patty in front of my position. I wedged my body under the dike so I couldn't be seen. The water was up to my nose. I lay back as far as I could while pushing my body into the mud bank of the rice patty dike. The grass gave me concealment. I could see my bunker and the one where the 81 guns were sitting because I'm outside the wire in a rice field. I was lying still and didn't move. My rifle was underwater, and my hand was on the trigger. Suddenly, my bunker was blown up. I heard Bishop scream. All hell had broken loose. The perimeter was being saturated with incoming fire from the VC. Mortar rounds and machine gunfire were hitting our positions from behind me in the tree line. The attack lasted about twenty minutes. I could feel the VC running across the top of the dike above my head.

Every few minutes, I could hear the footsteps above me, running fast. I could hear a marine calling for help. He said they were stabbing him. The sound above me was heavy, like someone being dragged. As they passed above me, I began to think of how to move without being noticed. My training told me to stay put and not to move. I sank lower in the water, up to my nose. I was planning on what to do because now it was quiet, and I was alone. I didn't know who survived the attack. I could hear only Vietnamese language; no American were talking. The VC had the village. I could see the 106 gun being carried off by the VC. The tent was on fire, and the VC was running around. I had made up my mind to move to where I had placed the claymore mine during the attack. I figured Bishop was dead because he was in the bunker, and he didn't follow me. Bishop was drunk and woke up, and he was in a fight, with the VC on top of him.

I knew what time it was when the VC attacked: 0130. I slowly looked at my watch. It was 0220. There was no movement above me, and it was dark. No Vietnamese voices. I decided that at 0300, I would move to the position where I placed that mine. I was prepared to fight when I moved from the rice patty.

I began to hear American voices and the rattling of gear hitting rifles. They went to the blown bunker. I could hear a voice calling out names. He said, "Dowell, you splib, where are you?" He called for Bishop. I knew they were part of our platoon because they called the right names. I answered up. He asked where I was. He said his name was Mulinger from weapons. I said, "If you aren't, I'm gonna blow you away." I went out of the dike and started toward the voices, and I could see Mulinger's white face and another marine. They helped me to my feet and said we had to find the rest by going to each position.

Someone was calling near the trees, and it was Bishop. He was shot in the ass. We found Gary Newton in the bushes with half of his leg gone, but he was still alive. Corporal Ruiz called out and crawled out of a ravine with a hole in his back. We made a 360 and put the wounded in the middle of us. Mulinger was giving the orders. I took Ruiz's cigarettes and took the clear cellophane off the pack and put the paper over the hole in his back to keep his lungs from collapsing. I lay on him until he got a shot of morphine. The cook came to use with a radio. He said the VC jumped him inside his shack. He said one had a grenade in his hand, and the cook killed him.

Mulinger got on the radio and called the regiment and told them what was happening at Antrack. The regiment was being attacked while he was radioing them. Mulinger called the battalion at Da Nang and got a response. Once he told them what happened, they told him help was on the way to us. He gave them the grid we were on, and the 55 battery shot white smoke rounds about two hundred yards out from us.

Mulinger told us they were going to saturate the area with 5.5 rounds from Da Nang. We had to stay down on the deck. The rounds came in. I had never been in bombardment before. I thought we were going to die from our own fire. They fired for a half hour, walking up to us and walking the round back and forth. It was loud and terrifying. I got scared then. After the firing was over, I could hear voices giving commands. The marines from the regiment had arrived. The medic came to us, and they put me on a truck on a stretcher. As they led me to the truck, they would say, "Here's another marine. He's dead." I looked down, and it was the marine from 81s whom I asked to go on watch at my position earlier that day. His back had a big hole where he had been shot, and his neck had been broken because his chest was on the deck and his head turned upward. When I saw him, I lost it. I really got scared after the fact. It all happened so quickly. I had not been scared until now. I just reacted to the situation. They put me on a truck and also put dead marines on there too.

THE UNITED STATES OF AMERICA

TO ALL WHO SHALL SEE THESE PRESENTS, GREETING:
THIS IS TO CERTIFY THAT
THE PRESIDENT OF THE UNITED STATES OF AMERICA
HAS AWARDED THE

PURPLE HEART

ESTABLISHED BY GENERAL GEORGE WASHINGTON
AT NEWBURGH, NEW YORK, AUGUST 7, 1782
TO

PRIVATE FIRST CLASS WILLIAM E. DOWELL, UNITED STATES MARINE CORPS

FOR WOUNDS RECEIVED
IN ACTION
REPUBLIC OF VIETNAM, 11 NOVEMBER 1966

GIVEN UNDER MY HAND IN THE CITY OF WASHINGTON
THIS   4TH   DAY OF   MARCH 2004

THE UNITED STATES OF AMERICA

TO ALL WHO SHALL SEE THESE PRESENTS, GREETING:
THIS IS TO CERTIFY THAT
THE PRESIDENT OF THE UNITED STATES OF AMERICA
HAS AWARDED THE

PURPLE HEART

ESTABLISHED BY GENERAL GEORGE WASHINGTON
AT NEWBURGH, NEW YORK, AUGUST 7, 1782
TO

PRIVATE FIRST CLASS WILLIAM E. DOWELL, UNITED STATES MARINE CORPS

FOR WOUNDS RECEIVED
IN ACTION
REPUBLIC OF VIETNAM, 12 NOVEMBER 1966

GIVEN UNDER MY HAND IN THE CITY OF WASHINGTON
THIS   4TH   DAY OF   MARCH 2004

They drove me to the chopper, and it took me to Da Nang Hospital. I was sore and had wounds all over my body. I couldn't see out of my left eye. At the hospital, they cut off my clothes and put a sheet over me. Two doctors came and told the sergeant, "Medivac these two. The plane leaves in twenty minutes." The doctor held up the sheet on me and said, "He needs surgery, but he won't die before you get him to another hospital. Send him to the Philippines." The sergeant told me that I was going home. He rushed me to the airstrip and loaded me on. They hooked the stretcher to straps hanging in the airplane. Bishop was across from me. His eye was black also. He said he was glad we had that fight.

A tall blond air force nurse came to me and called me Corporal Dowell. She said, "I'm going to give you shot to make the ride more comfortable for you." She gave a shot in the arm, and I went out.

23A

HEADQUARTERS
3rd Battalion, 1st Marines
1st Marine Division (Kein), FMF
FPO San Francisco 96602
17/WJK/jwm
5800

FOR OFFICIAL USE ONLY

From: Commanding Officer
To: Captain Leo J. KELLY 074957, U.S. Marine Corps

Subj: Investigation to inquire into the circumstances surrounding the attack on An Trach (1), Republic of Vietnam which occurred on or about 12 November 1966.

Ref: (a) JAG Manual

You are appointed to conduct an informal investigation in accordance with the provisions of part II of chapter VI of reference (a) concerning the attack on An Trach (1), Republic of Vietnam.

You will conduct a thorough investigation into all the circumstances connected with this incident and report your findings of fact, opinions, and recommendations, including any recommended administrative or disciplinary action.

Your duty to designate individuals as parties to the investigation during the proceedings is delineated in section 0302 of reference (a), you are empowered, but not required, to administer an oath to each witness attending to testify or depose during the course of the proceedings.

The original and ten copies of the investigation will be forwarded to the convening authority upon completion of the investigation.

H. F. De ATLEY

FOR OFFICIAL USE ONLY

Contact at
L. J. Kelly
7365 Annandale Ct
Annandale VA
22003

VARO/331
RECEIVED
MAY 19 2005
139
MAIL CLERK #6

FPO San Francisco 96602
LJK/jwm
5800
1 Dec 1966
From: Captain Leo J. KELLY 074957 United States Marine Corps
To: Commanding Officer, 3rd Battalion, 1st Marines

Subj: Investigation to inquire into the circumstances surrounding the Attack on An Trach (1), Republic of Vietnam which occurred on or about 12 November 1966

Ref: (a) JAG Manual

Encl:
(1) CO, 3rd Bn, 1st Mar appointing order 17/WJK/jwm over 5800 of 12 Nov 1966
(2) Map of An Trach (1)
(3) Listing of Weapons and equipment not recovered at An Trach (1)
(4) Statement of Major Sherman R. FOSTER, USA
(5) Statement of Captain Bradley F. CATE 072219 USMC
(6) Statement of 1st Lt. Charles T. SWEENEY 091062 USMC
(7) Statement of 2nd Lt. J. H. TERESTRA 091539 USMC
(8) Statement of 2nd Lt. David M. DEMMER 093899 USMCR
(9) Statement of SSgt. Toefua MAEVA 1348904 USMC
(10) Statement of Cpl. Joseph J. MEILINGER 2078241 USMC
(11) Statement of Cpl. Fernando RUIZ 1828929 USMC
(12) Statement of Cpl. Frank J. HILL 2073855 USMC
(13) Statement of Cpl. William D. BRYSON 2073725 USMC
(14) Statement of Cpl. Alfred E. SOCCORSO 2083212 USMC
(15) Statement of Cpl. James M. BOTHWELL JR. 2117978 USMC
(16) Statement of LCpl. Daniel R. GAUGHRAN 2030885 USMC
(17) Statement of LCpl. Thomas J. FARRELL 2145415 USMC
(18) Statement of LCpl. Charles D. SMITH 2119877 USMC
(19) Statement of LCpl. Curtis ROBINSON 2154442 USMC
(20) Statement of LCpl. Edward R. LANCE 2145235 USMC
(21) Statement of LCpl. Danny M. MCCAULEY 21011118 USMC

(22) Statement of LCpl. William T. DONAHUE 2183337 USMC

(23) Statement of LCpl. Eugene J. HALL 2030113 USMC

(24) Statement of LCpl. Thomas F. BANKS JR. 2105033 USMC

(25) Statement of LCpl. George M. KAUFFMAN 2246102 USMC

(26) Statement of LCpl. James P. ROSELEY 2109668 USMC

(27) Statement of LCpl. John RAVENELL 2105849 USMC

(28) Statement of PFC George M. KAUFFMAN 2246102 USMC

(29) Statement of PFC Alex HUGGINS 2242590 USMC

(30) Statement of PFC Nelson L. JOHNSON 2243835 USMC

(31) Statement of PFC Authur T. EVANS 2250235 USMC

(32) Statement of PFC Carl G. BURGY 2229249 USMC

(33) Statement of PFC Douglas W. WHITFIELD 2230071 USMC

(34) Statement of PFC Norman T. WYATT 2267088 USMC

(35) Statement of PFC Joseph E. DYKES 2055052 USMC

(36) Statement of PFC Jerry E. BROWN 2260762 USMC

(37) Statement of PFC David E. LAMBERT 2269648 USMC

(38) Statement of PFC David F. JOHNSON 2216662 USMC

(39) Statement of PFC James E. DAKE 2191554 USMC

(40) Statement of PFC Paul R. MCNEIL 2280209 USMC

(41) Statement of PFC Dallas R. LAY 2152416 USMC

(42) Statement of LCpl. Larry A. KIMMY 2154493 USMC

(43) Statement of PFC Gary R. BOYETT 2069071 USMC

(44) Statement of Pvt. Troung van LONG 203065 ARVN

(45) Statement of PFC Ho TUONG 200999 ARVN

(46) Statement of Pvt. Phan Nguo LONG ARVN

(47) Statement of Vo MAN, PAT member

(48) Statement of Cpl. Tran KY 014380 ARVN

(49) Statement of Cpl. Tran Thanh NY 205972 ARVN

(50) Statement of Pvt. Nguyan Huu NIEM 202945 ARVN

(51) Statement of Dang BIEN, PAT Leader and village chief

(52) Statement of Tray MUOI, PAT member

(53) Statement of Trong Doi VY, PAT member

(54) Statement of Tran Diem DUY, PAT member

(55) Statement of Le VAN TA, PAT member

(56) Statement of Nguyen Huo LAU, PAT member

(57) Statement of Dang MOT, Hoa Khanh Catholic Refugee
Camp, RVN

(58) Statement of Dang THAI, Hoa Khanh Catholic Refugee
Camp, RVN

(59) Statement of Le Huu KHAI, Hoa Khanh Catholic Refugee
Camp, RVN

(60) Statement of Dang MOI, Hoa Khanh Catholic Refugee
Camp, RVN

(61) Statement of Dang Thi THANHI, Khanh Catholic Refugee
Camp, RVN

(62) Statement of Le HONG, Hoa Khanh Catholic Refugee
Camp, RVN

Preliminary Statement

Pursuant to the provisions of enclosure (1) and in accordance with
reference (a) an investigation was initiated on 12 November 1966
to inquire into the circumstances surrounding the attack on An
Trach (1), Republic of Vietnam which occurred on or about 12
November 1966.

There were some difficulties encountered during the investigation in
acquiring statements from witnesses. An interpreter, Staff Sergeant
Nguyen Dong MINH, aided in interviewing the Vietnamese nation-
als, Republic of Vietnam soldiers, and the members of the political action team stationed at An Trach (1), Quang Nam Province,
Republic of Vietnam. Several of the marine witnesses were so seri-
ously wounded that they were evacuated before they were able to
make the statements or made statements under medication and in
extreme pain, others were evacuated prior to signing their statements. No other difficulties were encountered during the conduc-
tion of this investigation and I believe that no pertinent facts regard-
ing the attack can be ascertained by speaking with those witnesses
not now available.

A note is included to explain the term PAT. Throughout the investigation the term PAT was used to describe members of the political action team stationed at An Trach (1). The proper name for the group is Rural Development Cadre. However, few witnesses used this term, so the investigation always refers to those persons as PATs.

Findings of Fact

That the Third Platoon of India Company, reinforced with one 106 Recoilless Rifle and one section of 81MM Mortars was located at the village of An Trach (1), Quang Nam Province, Republic of Vietnam on 12 November 1966 (see enclosures (5), (6), and (8)).

That the Third Platoon of India Company, reinforced, consisted of sixty men, one marine officer, fifty-seven marine enlisted and two corpsmen (see enclosure (8)).

That Second Lieutenant David M. DEMMER 093899/0301 U.S. Marine Corps Reserve was the platoon commander of the Third Platoon of India Company (see enclosure (5) and (8)).

That a twenty-two man platoon from the 1st Battalion, 51st ARVN Regiment was located at the village of An Trach (1) on 12 November 1966 (see enclosure (4)).

That forty-two members of a political action team from Hoa Vang District Headquarters were located in the village of An Trach (1) on 12 November 1966 (see enclosure (4)).

That the village of An Trach (1) is located at grid coordinates 972662m Map She_____6658 IV, Series L701, USA Map Service, Corps of Engineers 1/50,000 1962.

That sometime prior to 0200 on 12 November 1966 an insurgent (Viet Cong) force of unknown strength infiltrated the marine defensive position at An Trach (1) (see enclosures (5) through (62)).

That a marine patrol had set up an ambush and patrolled the area to the southeast of An Trach (1) between the hours of 111900H and 120045H (see enclosure (12)).

That the marine patrol had discovered nothing unusual in the area to the southeast of An Trach (1) (see enclosures (6), (8), and (12)).

That sometime in the late morning and early afternoon of 11 November 1966 the marine position on the western side of An Trach (1) received heavy small arms fire from the west and northwest (see enclosures (6), (8), and (51)).

That from 1800 to 2200 each night the marines are on a 100% watch, and that from 2200 until daylight the marines switched to 50% watch (see enclosure (8)).

That the marines on post the evening and morning of 11 and 12 November 1966 were especially alert because of the heavy volume of small arms fire received that afternoon (see enclosures (8) through (43)).

That the defensive positions at An Trach (1) numbered fourteen on 12 November 1966 (see enclosures (2) and (8)).

That the distance between the defensive positions at An Trach (1) varied from thirty to one hundred meters (see enclosures (2)).

That the platoon radio operators had their radio installed in the platoon command post position (see enclosures (8), (9), and (33)).

That the positions manned by the U. S. Marines and the ARVN troops were the same positions that they manned every night for the last five months (see enclosures (8), and (51)).

That the 81MM mortar section had their radio up on the 81 conduct of fire net and it was located with the 81MM mortar section (see enclosures (16) and (33)).

That at approximately 0200 12 November 1966 the 1st Battalion, 11th Marines received 25 incoming 81MM mortar rounds at their position which is located at grid coordinates AT 987675. These rounds were fired from grid coordinates AT 988670 which is approximately 500 meters north of An Trach (1) (see enclosure (6) and (7)).

That at approximately 0200 12 November 1966 the defensive positions, the platoon command post and the 81MM mortar sections positions at An Trach (1) were attacked by an unknown number of Viet Cong (see enclosure (5) and (56)).

The posts 8, 9, 10, 11, 12, and 14 on the western side of the perimeter were not attacked but did receive a few rounds of small arms.

That the Viet Cong attacked the positions from within the defensive perimeter using satchel charges, hand grenades, C-4 charges and small _____ fire (see enclosures (6) through (43)).

That the marine force at An Trach (1) lost or had captured by the insurgents numerous items of arms and equipment (see enclosure (3)).

That the soldiers from the 1st Battalion, 51st Army of the Republic of Vietnam regiment had the following weapons captured during the attack at An Trach (1) on 12 November 1966 (see enclosure (49)):

M-79 with 50 rounds of ammunition
M-1 rifle

That the political action team at An Trach (1) had the following weapons captured during the attack on An Trach (1) on 12 November 1966 (see enclosure (53)):

6 M-1 or M-2 carbines
1 .45 caliber pistol
1 sub machines gun (type unknown)

That the marine forces suffered the following casualties during the attack on An Trach (1) on 12 November 1966 (see enclosure (45)):

15 killed in action (1 navy, 14 marine corps)
28 wounded in action (1 navy, 27 marine corps)

That the army of the Republic of Vietnam suffered the following casualties during the attack on An Trach (1) and 12 November 1966:

1 killed in action
1 missing in action
6 wounded in action (see enclosure (45))

That the political action team at An Trach (1) had one man wounded in action (see enclosure (5)).

That the company executive officer could not raise the Third Platoon of India Company on the company tactical net at 0200 on 12 November 1966 (see enclosure (6)).

That the 81MM mortar platoon could not raise the mortar section at An Trach (1) on the 81MM conduct of fire net at 0200 12 November 1966 (see enclosure (6)).

That at 0245 the 1st Battalion, 11th Marines received a transmission on their conduct of fire net from a radio operator with the 81MM mortar section at An Trach (1) (information supplied investigating officer) (see enclosures (5) and (6)).

That the radio operator reported that they had been overrun and suffered many casualties (see Enclosure (6)).

That the marines at An Trach (1) killed approximately seven Viet Cong. Three bodies were found and four more were seen being carried off (see enclosure (6) and (5)).

That at approximately 0400 12 November 1966 a relief force from 1st Marines and Company I, 3rd Battalion, 1st Marines entered the village.

That the political action team did not fight during the attack on An Trach (1) (see enclosure (47), (51) through (56)).

That the political action team members did not attack or resist the Viet Cong during the early morning of 12 November 1966 (see enclosures (47), (51) through (56)).

That during the attack the members of the political action team hid in houses, foxholes, bomb shelters and any other place they could find concealment (see enclosures (47), (51) through (56)).

That no witnesses to the attack on An Trach (1) know how the Viet Cong entered the perimeter (see enclosures (8) through (62)).

That no witnesses to the attack at An Trach (1) know how the Viet Cong escaped from the perimeter (see enclosures (8) through (62)).

That the radios utilized by the Third Platoon of India Company were disbursed by at least seventy-five meters (see enclosures (8), (16), and (33).

That radio communications to higher headquarters was lost due to the destruction of the two radio positions simultaneously (see enclosures (6), (8), and (33)).

That no one questioned concerning this attack had any forewarning of an ensuing attack (see enclosures (5) though (62)).

That the people of the village did not know the attack was going to occur on 12 November 1966 (see enclosures (51) through (62)).

That it was a dark overcast night and visibility was extremely poor (knowledge of the investigating officer).

Opinions

That the attack on An Trach (1) by the Viet Cong was well planned, coordinated and executed.

That the Viet Cong infiltrated the marine position somewhere through the northeast portion of the perimeter.

That the Viet Cong force was approximately 35 to 50 men strong.

That the signal to execute the attack was the 81MM mortar rounds fired on the 1st Battalion, 11th Marines.

That the attack lasted no more than thirty minutes.

That if the ARVN soldiers and PATs would have reacted more aggressively, their assistance could have resulted in repelling the attackers.

That the Viet Cong withdrew to the northeast of An Trach (1).

Recommendations

That in each regiment, battalion, company and platoon position a four-man team be continually employed as a patrol within the perimeter during the hours of darkness of restricted visibility.

That fixed bunkers around a perimeter have manned fighting holes adjacent to them.

LISTING OF WEAPONS AND EQUIPMENT
NOT RECOVERED AT AN TRACH (1)

Rifle M-14, 7.62MM	TOTAL NOT RECOVERED 16	
PFC N. L. JOHNSON	918840	
CPL D. D. YARNELL	423505	
CPL R. FERNANDO	1057077	
PFC A. H. SHIELDS	456402	
PFC E. G. NEWTON	145302	
LCPL C. E. MEEK	430906	
LCPL C. ROBINSON	812948	
PFC G. M. KAUFFMAN	803729	
PFC T. D. BROOMFIELD	114669	
PFC R. G. ALVIS	1156518	
PFC G. R. BOYETT	1360607	
LCPL L. D. DEFILIPPIS	568834	
PVT D. E. LAMBERT	1381016	
LCPL D. M. MCCAULEY	1167819	
LCPL D. R. GAUGHRAN	815923	
LCPL J. P. BROWN	1164415	
PISTOL CALIBER .45	TOTAL NOT RECOVERED 9	
CP. F. J. HILL	749558	
LT D. A. DEMMER	1350613	
CPL R. L. POWELL	2638013	
SSGT MAEVA	874596	
PFC D. ACOSTA	2627827	
LCPL T. J. FARREL	239772	
PFC D. W. WHITFIELD	1996159	
HN J. B. LEE	2629658	
HN M. AVILA JR.	2634317	
81MM MORTAR BARREL	8074	TOTAL LOST:

81MM MORTAR BIPON	1390	TOTAL LOST:
M-60 MACHINE GUN	65049	TOTAL LOST:
ELEVATION MECHANISM	7792990	TOTAL LOST:
ACCESSORY PACK	N/A	TOTAL LOST:
CLAYMORE MINES		TOTAL LOST:
TA-1	1664	TOTAL LOST:
TA-2	1904	TOTAL LOST:

THE FOLLOWING COMMUNICATIONS
GEAR WAS DESTROYED:

TA - 1	1501
TA - 1	5190

STATEMENT OF MAJOR SHEERMAN R. FOSTER, U.S. ARMY, SENIOR ADVISOR HOA VANG SUBSECTOR, REPUBLIC OF VIETNAM

22 November 1966

There are 52 personnel assigned to the cadre team at An Trach. On 12 November 1966 there were 42 cadre present for duty. Nine cadre were on leave, one cadre was in Hoi An to pick up his weapon. Questioning of the cadre leader indicates that all 42 men were present for duty in the hamlet. Three of the cadre were in the command post area talking with the marines. The remainder were billeted immediately adjacent to the command post. The marine platoon and ARVN platoon have been stationed in An Trach since my arrival in Hoa Vang on 15 July 1966. There is no one presently assigned to this headquarters that can____

The above information is correct to the best of my knowledge.

SHERMAN R. FOSTER

STATEMENT OF CAPTAIN BRADLEY F. CATE
072219/0302/0202 U.S. MAINE CORPS

12 November 1966

I, Captain Bradley F. Cate 072219/0303/0202 USMC, having been informed by Captain Leo J. Kelly of the matter under investigation and having first been advised of my rights under Article 31b of the Uniform Code of Military Justice do hereby voluntarily make the following statement:

On the morning of 12 November 1966, at approximately 0100 I-6 failed to receive a radio check from I-3. I-3 was located within and around the hamlet of An Trach (1) coordinates 969654. Their mission was to defend the hamlet. After several attempts to reach I-3 by radio, plans were made to move a squad of 60 M. mortar personnel to An Trach. At approximately 0300 word was received from Regiment COC that An Trach had been mortared. One of the 81MM men at An Trach had found their radio and had come up on the conduct of fire net. With troops from Regiment and Company I, I moved into An Trach. This was approximately 0400. Things were in pretty bad shape. It was very, very dark, and was raining heavily. The church was used to treat the WIAs, and set up a CP. Three 6 by 6 trucks were brought in and the WIAs were sent to regiment. Then the KIAs were sent out. As light came, we then could figure out what had happened. It is my opinion that approximately 20 to 25 Viet Cong were already in the hamlet. That they had been there planning and rehearsing their mission for at least one month. Approximately six different positions were blown at the same time. (1) CP (2) 81MM mortars (3) 106s school house (5) two gun positions (6) corpsman quarters. With approximately six other positions grenade. All positions had small or unused plus grenades. Many charges of different sizes were found in the area. At no place did I find any wire around An Trach having been breached. It was definitely an inside job. Taking approximately 20 minutes. In talking with the troops, most of them only saw one, maybe two Viet Cong. Three Viet Cong bodies were found all carrying charges and grenades on them. They wore only shorts. At the time of the attack, there was supposed to ARVN from the 1st for the fifty-first PFs, and approximately 25 to 30 body guards for the hamlet chief, Mr. Bien. All the marines I talked to stated they saw none of these people around. Nowhere did I find where the Viet Cong mortars were used. Total WIas-28 (1 USN), 15 KIAs, (_USN).

BRADLEY F. CATE

_side. As the marines casualties were being loaded on to trucks and evacuate. I organized a detail to check the perimeter. Post # 13 had been hit from the front and from the read. According to Private First Class Wyatt, he was awoken by small ertis fire directed at his position from outside the perimeter. As he got up he heard something rattling, coming toward his bunker from inside the perimeter. It was a Vietnamese wearing a light green uniform and no cover. At first Wyatt thought the Vietnamese was an ARVN, but when he reached the rear of his bunker, he threw a grenade. This grenade was a dud and a gun battle ensued. During the fight and caused heavy damage to the bunker but did not cause any marine casualties. Post # 14 didn't show signs of being engaged whereas post 1, 2, 3, 4, 5, and 6 reflected close in combat. At bunker one I found Private First Class Broomfield in front of his sleeping couch on his back with his right leg bent at the knee up under his body.

There were no visible wounds, but he complained of having feeling his lower _____. He was carried to the church on a wooden stretcher and died approximately an hour later. At post #2, I found Lambert manning the 106 and Private First Cass Bozette in the sleeping hatch. They both were highly nervous and in a slight state of shock. Lance Corporal Dephillips had been shot and decapitated by an explosive near the MG emplacement. Another member of the 106 section was found shot in Mama Son's and Papa Son's yard a short distance from Dephillips. The sleeping was within a tree line, and was hit from inside the perimeter. The 106 emplacement which was about 30 meters out in a rice paddy was not engaged. At Post #5 I found two marines killed in action. Corporal Powell was blown to death while sleeping in his rack. Another marine appeared to have been dragged from the position and discarded in the brush approximately 25 meters away. From personal observations, of the area, and conversations with the defenders I am convinced that the communist insurgent forces utilizing satchel charges, and grenades automatic weapons, and semiautomatic rifle fire initiated their assault from within the perimeter. This is further substantiated by the fact I found Chi-Chon 7.62 shell casings, Chi-Chon grenades, and blocks of C-4, rigged for detonation inside the perimeter. I personally saw and checked out two dead Viet Cong. One was found off the trail near post #3 and appeared to have died of wounds about the head; presumably from accidental self-detonation of one of his homemade grenades. The other Viet Cong was found between the mess hall and church. He had his upper right side of his head blown away. He had been shot at close range with an M-14 rifle by Private First Class Smith.

CHARLES T. SWEENEY
(ENCL 6)

VARO/0331
RECEIVED

MAY 19 2005 139
MAIL CLERK#3

STATEMENT OF SECOND LIEUTENANT J. H TERPSTRA JR. 091539, U.S. MARINE CORPS, WHISKEY BATTERY, 1ST BATTALION, 11TH MARINES

12 November 1966

I, Second Lieutenant J. H. Terpstra Jr 091539 USMC having been informed by Captain Leo J. Kelly of the mater under investigation and having been first advised of my rights under Article 31b of the Uniform Code of Military Justice do hereby voluntarily make the following statement:

The following information in known by me to be true. On 12 November 1966 at approximately 0200 hours the 1st Battalion, 11th Marines located at grid coordinates AT 987675 received 16 incoming 81MM mortar rounds. Crater analysis teams from Headquarters Battery, Whiskey Battery and Lima Battery determined by taking back azimuths that the rounds were fired from the general area of grid coordinates AT 988670.

J. H. TERPSTRA
(ENCLO 7)

STATEMENT OF 2ND LT. DAVID___DEMMER
093899/0-01, U.S. MARINE CORPS

19 November 1966

I, 2nd Lt. David __ Demmer 093899/0301 USMC, having been informed by Captain Leo H. Kelly of the matter under investigation and having first been advised of my rights under Article 31b of the Uniform Code of Military Justice do hereby voluntarily make the following statement:

On the night of 11 November 1966, I was in my command post located in the village of An Trach. There was sixty men assigned to this post including two corpsman. On the morning of the attack 1 was awakened by the initial explosion. I immediately contacted Staff Sergeant Maeva and he said we were being mortared. The next thing I remembered was Maeva yelling that he was hit. I then ran to the next road and saw the right guide pinned under some rubble. Jimmy, one of the Vietnamese boys we used as an interpreter, was in the radio room. He was killed in the initial explosion. The afternoon prior to the attack, we received a heavy volume of small arms fire along our northern perimeter, we received a heavy volume of small arms fire along our northern perimeter. I proceeded to post #12, to check it out and decided to call in on 81's fire mission. That afternoon at the squad leaders meeting I passed on all the information I'd had, none of which contained a hint of an ensuing enemy attack. Due to the size of our perimeter and the number of personnel assigned to guard it there was often difficulty trying to man our posts and supply patrols for our area at the same time. We have fourteen posts on the perimeter. The area surrounding post #14 being the most insecure. The ARVN soldiers were assigned along with two marines to posts #3 and 14. The lieutenant in charge of the ARVN was responsible for post #6. Each squad leader was responsible for _____ timely checks on his respective posts. After the altercation along our northern perimeter, I personally checked the post that afternoon. That night the squad leaders were instructed to check posts. We maintained a

100% watch until 2200 each evening, then it was 50% until the next morning. The 81s maintained a radio watch 24 hours per day. The 106 position is manned at all times. We placed claymore lines out in the vicinity of posts #1, 3, and 14 during the hours of darkness and took them in at first light. It was my desire to cut down some of the trees to make the fields of fire, however my request was rejected by the village chief. In some areas visual contact with adjacent posts was impossible cue to the heavy foliage. During the attack I had idea of the whereabouts of either Mr. Bien, the village chief or any of the ARVNs.

DAVID __. DEMMER
(ENCL 8)

STATEMENT OF STAFF SERGEANT TOEFUA MAEVA
1348904/0369 U.S. MARINE CORPS

12 November 1966

I, Staff Sergeant Toefua Maeva 1348904/0369 USMC, having been informed by Captain Leo J. Kelly of the matter under investigation and having first been advised of my rights under Article 31b of the Uniform Code of Military Justice do hereby voluntarily make the following statement:

I was awake at a proximately 2400 on 11 November 1966, when a previously reported ambush patrol came in. I did not feel too good that day so I went down to my rack and laid down. About 0100 I was in the rack and I heard an explosion in our building and I was knocked unconscious. I came to and started to help the radio operator. It was here that I was shot in the chest by an automatic weapon. I could not move so I laid in the building until help came and took us to the 81's position. We stayed there until the relief column arrived and took us to regiment for medical care and further transportation to NSA.

TOEFUA MAEVA
(ENCLO 9)

STATEMENT OF CORPORAL JOESPH J. MULLINGER
2078241 1/0311 U.S. MARINE CORPS

13 November 1966

I, Corporal Joseph J. Mullinger 2078241/0311 USMC, having been informed by Captain Leo J. Kelly of the matter under investigation and having first advised of my rights under Article 31b of the Uniform Code of Military Justice do hereby voluntarily make the following statement:

I was the squad leader on post #12 at the time of the attack. The Viet Cong opened up with satchel charges to our rear, inside the perimeter. I waited to see if they were coming to our position. The Lance Corporal Kinmy and I went to posts #8, 9, 10, to see how they were. It was in this vicinity that a Viet Cong fired and hit me in the hip. Lance Corporal Kinmy killed him. We then went to posts #8, 9, 10, we went into the 81's area and commenced aiding the wounded and established a perimeter. We held this position until relief came to which time I was evacuated to regimental headquarters then to NSA.

JOESPH J. MULLINGER

Corporal Joesph J. Mullinger was located in C Med at the time this statement was made. He has since been evacuated out of the Republic of Vietnam. Certified to be a true statement of the above named individual.

L. J. KELLY
Captain USMC
(ENCL 10)

Witnessed by

W. J. KANE JR.
2nd Lt. USMC

STATEMENT OF CORPORAL FERNANDO RUIZ
1828929/0311 U.S. MARINE CORPS

13 November 1966

I, Corporal Fernando Ruiz 1828929/0311 USMC having been informed by Captain Leo J. Kelly of the matter under investigation and having first advised of my rights under Article 31b of the Uniform Code of Military Justice do hereby voluntarily make the following statement.

I remember the building I was in being hit from inside the perimeter. I was shot in the back, and remember the building falling in on me. The next thing I can recall was a Viet Cong standing over me asking me to surrender, I blacked out. I came to and tried to free myself from the debris which had covered me when the building exploded. Help arrived soon after and freed me and carried me to the 81's perimeter. It think the V. C. came through in the vicinity of post 4. I don't know where my rifle is, it was in the building when it exploded.

FERNANDO RUIZ

Corporal Fernando Ruiz was located in C Med at the time this statement was made. He has since been evacuated out of the Republic of Vietnam. Certified to be a true statement of the above named individual.

L. J. KELLY
Capt. USMC
(ENCL 11)

Witnessed by

W. J. KANE JR.   VARO/331
2nd Lt. USMC   RECEIVED
          MAY 19 2005 139
          MAIL CLERK #6

Cpl. Ruiz was with me at the time I was wounded, he received V.A. benefits. Please contact him. I was at Med C, also—evacuated out Chut Med Regiment.

STATEMENT OF CORPORAL FRANK J. HILL
2073855/0311 U.S. MARINE CORPS

12 November 1966

I Corporal Frank J. Hill 2073855/0311 USMC, having been informed by Captain Leo J. Kelly of the matter under investigation and having first been advised of my rights under Article 31b of the Uniform Code of Military Justice do hereby voluntarily make the following statement:

I returned from a night ambush abut 0045. I was in charge of the patrol. Everything was quiet. When I got back I went to the C. P. with the radio men and checked in. Private First Class Johnson was my radio man. When I got back to post #6, I told the men who relieved us for the patrol to go back to their positions. I smoked a cigarette and laid down, started going toward the doorway. I had an M-79 and a pistol. Corporal Ruiz ran out the door. At first I saw him scream and then he fell back through the doorway. I started for the door, then I saw something come through it. At first I thought it was a grenade. It was fizzling. I thought it was a dud, so I never give it another thought, and started for the door, but it went off. Then all the bricks fell on top of me. I was there ten minutes before I got the bricks off us. I heard post #5 scream to post #6, so I went down there. I saw PFC Newton lying in the brush. He was hurt so bad, he could not move his arms or legs. So I pulled him out of the bushes. Corporal Mullinger, Corporal Bryson, PFC Johnson, and somebody else started yelling down to us. We told them that we needed help. They came down and carried Newton away on a blanket. We picked up all the cartridge belts and rifles we could find and set up a perimeter there at 81's. I didn't see any V. C. I figure Ruiz got it as he was going out the door, because I heard an incoming round and then where the V. C. came from. I did not see any ARVN during the attack, nor were they manning the post when I was there. They could have been buried under but I didn't see them. I thought at first we were being lettered. I have a .45 caliber pistol. It is buried at the school under the rubble. I heard the V. C., but I couldn't see them. I heard them hollering. One was calling for another one. I heard them by 106's laughing and screaming. My rifle # is 8129409-14 modified.

FRANK J. HILL
(ENCLO 12)

STATEMENT OF CORPORAL WILLIAM D. BRYSON 2073725/0351, U.S. MARINE CORPS

12 November 1966

I, Corporal William D. Bryson 2073725/0351 USMC, having been informed by Captain Leo J. Kelly of the matter under investigation and having first been advised of my rights under Article 31b of the Uniform Code of Military Justice do hereby voluntarily make the following statement:

At approximately 0130 one of my men woke me up. I got shrapnel in the face that day, and it wasn't my turn to go on guard, so he went to wake the other man up and I laid back down. I was on post 10. There is one man on post at all times on this post to make sure the no one comes through the perimeter. Private First Class Paoletti was on post at the time of the incident. He was on his way down to wake his relief up when the Viet Cong hit. Everything happened in a matter of seconds. All the mortar rounds went off. No more than five minutes later Corporal Heillinger came down the path. At that time we went around to all posts to try and reorganize and find out what the story was. We went down to post 9 to see if anybody was there. Post 9 was alright. We went down the line to post 12 and the rest of posts. Post 7 was unmanned. Jonsson from post 6 told us to come on down one of the men was wounded. One man was trapped in the school, we sent two man there to dig him out. Myself and Corporal Heillinger continued up to post 5. I hear a man call me from the brush of post 4. Some of the men there were wounded so we took them back to the command post. I took some men to check post 5, but they told me the man there was dead. Post 7 was always an ARVN bunker, and was unmanned. The lieutenant and the corporal of the guard usually check the lines. They usually check the lines two or three times a night. My weapon is an M-14 automatic rifle. After we went to post 6, the men were all hurt pretty bad, we dropped a man again. At this time posts 10, 9 and 8 were the only posts we knew of that were not hit. Then we went up to the command post. I went to see how bad the lieutenant's wounds were, he was pretty bad, he had at least three chest wounds and there was a nick in his head. Sergeant maeva was lying there, he said that he was OK and for me to check the radio man. I walked in another room and found a man sprawled across a .50 caliber, he was dead. Then I walked into the radio shack and found "Lelch" and Shields, they were both dead. I also saw the Vietnamese kid. He didn't have a head. Lieutenant Sweeney came in and took over from there. I did not see or shoot any Viet Cong. I have no idea how the Viet Cong got in the perimeter. On the afternoon of 11 November 1966 we got hit from across the river. That evening we were told to be especially watchful. We had a feeling we were going to be hit again.

WILLIAM D. BRYSON
(ENCL 13)

STATEMENT OF CORPORAL JAMES R. BOTHWWELL JR. 2117278/0311, U.S. MAINE CORPS

13 November 1966

I, Corporal James R. Bothwell Jr. 2117978/0311 USMC, having been informed by Captain Leo J. Kelly of the matter under investigation and having been first advised of my rights under Article 31b of the Uniform Code of Military Justice do hereby voluntarily make the following statement:

I was sleeping at the time of the initial attack. I was blown from my rack and thrown out of the tent. I tried to crawl to the gun position but was hit by shrapnel and knocked unconscious. The next thing I remember I was here in NSA. We did not fire any concentration that night.

JAMES R. BOTHWELL JR.

Corporal James R. Bothwell was located in C Med at the time this statement was made. He has since been evacuated out of the Republic of Vietnam. Certified to be a true statement of the above named individual.

L. J. KELLY
Captain USMC
Encl (15)

Witnessed by

W. J. KANE JR.
2nd Lt. USMC

STATEMENT OF LANCE
CORPORAL DANIEL R. GAUGHRAN
2030885/0341, U.S. MARINE CORPS

13 November 1966

I, Lance Corporal Daniel R. Gaughran 2030885/0341 USMC having been informed by Captain Leo J. Kelly of the matter under investigation and having been first advised of my right under Article 31b of the Uniform Code of Military Justice do hereby voluntarily make the following statement:

I was the radio watch with 81's section the night of the attack. I was blown from the tent during the initial blast on our position. I tried to get up and return to the radio but was shot at close range I remember I was being brought into NSA Hospital.

DANIEL R. GAUGHRAN

Lance Corporal Daniel R. Gaughran was located in NSA at the time this statement was made. He has since been evacuated out of the Republic of Vietnam. Certified to be a true statement of the above named individual.

L. J. KELLY
ENCL (16)

Witnessed by

W. J. KANE JR.
2nd Lt. USMC

STATEMENT OF LANCE CORPORAL THOMAS J. FARRELL 2145415/0341, U.S. MARINE CORPS

13 November 1966

I, Lance Corporal Thomas J. Farrell 2145415/0341 having been informed by Captain Leo J. Kelly of the matter under investigation and having been first advised of my rights under Article 31b of the Uniform Code of Military Justice do hereby voluntarily make the following statement:

I was sleeping in 81's tent when the attack occurred. I was blown from my rack in the initial explosion. The Viet Cong were running everywhere inside the perimeter, they were wearing pajamas and looked like they were wearing soft covers on their heads. I do not know where the ARVN were but after the Viet Cong left the PFs came and were trying to help us. The attack lasted a total of about 45 minutes. I was wounded in the initial attack and Private First Class Smith came in the 81's area and took my weapon. It was soon after this that Corporal Bryson came into the area and set up a hasty defense. I was later evacuated to NSA Hospital.

THOMAS J. FARRELL

Lance Corporal Thomas J. Farrell was located in NSA at the time this statement was made. He has since been evacuated out of the Republic of Vietnam. Certified to be a true statement of the above named individual.

L. J. KELY
Capt. USMC

Witnessed by

W. J. KANE JR.
2nd Lt. USMC

STATEMENT OF LANCE CORPORAL CHARLES D. SMITH
2319877/3371 U.S. MARINE CORPS

13 November 1966

I, Lance Corporal Charles D. Smith 2119877/3371 USMC having been informed by Captain Leo J. Kelly of the matter under investigation and having been first advised of my rights under Article 31b of the Uniform Code of Military Justice do hereby voluntarily make the following statement:

I was sleeping in the mess hall when the explosion started. I jumped out of the rack and ran outside. I ran into a Viet Cong, we strangled, I strangled him then ran back to the house to get my pants and rifle. I ran back out and shot the Viet Cong I had struggled with. It was at this time my rifle exploded. I ran toward the command post area, there were about 20 Viet Cong running around. I did not see any ARVN or PATs at the time of the attack. After the attack I saw two or three PFs trying to help the wounded. The Viet Cong were dressed in shorts and had two baskets tied on their sides to carry their charges in. I was wounded in the head during the attack and was taken to "C" Med for medical treatment.

CHARLES D. SMITH
ENCL (18)

STATEMENT OF LANCE CORPORAL BURTIS ROBINSON 2154442/0311 U.S. MARINE CORPS

13 November 1966

I, Lance Corporal Curtis Robinson 2154442/0311 USMC having been informed by Captain Leo J. Kelly of the matter of under investigation and having first been advised of my rights under Article 31b of the Uniform Code of Military Justice do hereby voluntarily make the following statement:

I was on post 6 at the time of the attack. There were 4 men with me. I was on watch at the time. I heard fire and explosions in the command post area and there was a lot of yelling. I heard the Viet Cong talking, then there was a lot an explosion and the building fell in on me. The Viet Cong were coming over the bridge. I remember one of them stepping on my hand while I was buried under the rubble. I freed myself then tried to free Ruiz. Corporal Bryson then came and helped take wounded to the command post. We waited until relief came then were evacuated to "C" Med.

CURTIS ROBINSON

Corporal Curtis Robinson was located in "C" Med at the time this statement was made. He has since been evacuated out of the Republic of Vietnam. Certified to be a true statement of the above named individual.

L. J. KELLY
ENCL (19)

Witnessed by

W. J. KANE JR.
2nd Lt. USMC

STATEMENT OF LANCE CORPORAL EDWARD R. LANCE
2145235/0311, U.S. MARINE CORPS

12 November 1966

I, Lance Corporal Edward R. Lance 2145235/0311, USMC, having been informed by Captain Leo J. Kelly of the matter under investigation and having firsst been advised of my rights under Article 31b of the Uniform Code of Military Justice do hereby voluntarily make the following statement.

About 0100 12 November 1966, we just came off ambush. Our squad leader told us to go back to our holes and relieve the men that had relieved us for the ambush patrol. My post was #8, we took over post #8 there were three of us in the post. Mcneil had the first watch. Just before the attack we were lying down trying to go to sleep. I don't know why I couldn't go to sleep. I had no idea that there was going to be an attack. When the attack began, I thought that we were being mortared. I did not see any Viet Cong, except for the dead ones. Nobody shot at us the 81 mortars did not fire that night

EDWARD R. LANCE
ENCL (20)

STATEMENT OF LANCE CORPORAL DANNY M. MCCAULEY, 2101118/0341, U.S. MARINE CORPS

12 November 1966

I, Lance Corporal Danny M. Mccauley, USMC, having been informed by Captain Leo J. Kelly of the matter under investigation and having first been advised of my rights under Article 31b of the Uniform Code of Military Justice do hereby voluntarily make the following statement:

I am an A-Gunner in 81 mortars, attached to the third platoon of India Company. At 0130 hours, 12 November 1966, I was sleeping in my rack outside of 81's tent, just across the street from I Company's command post. The India (3) Command Post is located in An Trach (1) Village. I was not on watch this morning of 12 November. I was sleeping I looked for my rifle, but it wasn't there. I saw about four or five V. C. It looked like they were pulling pins on grenades and throwing them at us. Corporal Bothwell told us to get on the guns. When we were running to the guns a couple of guys got hurt pretty bad, that was when the grenades came in on us, and I got shrapnel in the leg and face. I heard Corporal Bothwell yell, "Somebody help me. I can't see." We took Bothwelll back to what was left of the 815 tent. The Viet Cong then started running through the command post shooting people. PFC Whitfield was trying to find someone on the radio net. He finally got somebody and asked for help. Then about 30 minutes later a corporal came. I don't know his name, but he picked up a few guys to see if they could help anyone that was still out there. There was only us and some of 81's left, so we set up a perimeter and one by one the wounded kept coming in. We finally got contact with a patrol that was coming out from regiment approach. They fired a cluster, and about halfway down the road, they arranged signal. When they got to the command post, they helped us with the wounded. At the time of the incident, I was firing a .45 caliber pistol. I do not know where my rifle went. My rifle # was 1167819, and is automatic rifle, with bipods on it. I looked for it later. A few rifles were found but mine was not with them. I was not on watch that night. We usually catch watch every second night with a night off in between. We are well rested when we assume post. Two marines stand post with the ARVN. We have four ARVN. The ARVN stayed on post all night, I am sure that they were there. After we were hit four or five ARVN came into the perimeter. I didn't know them, they usually change every other night.

DANNY M. MCCAULEY
ENCL (21)

STATEMENT OF LANCE CORPORAL WILLIAM T. DONAHUE 2183 37/0331, U.S. MARINE CORPS

12 November 1966

I, Lance Corporal William T. Donahue 2183337/0331 USMC, having been informed by Captain Leo J. Kelly of the matter under investigation and having first been advised of my right under Article 31b of the Uniform Code of Military Justice do hereby voluntarily make the following statement.

I returned from a night ambush patrol about 0300. About 0115 we were setting up on our bunker getting ready to set the watch. That was when the first explosion occurred. We couldn't get any radio contact with the C. P. Word was passed not to fire unless we had a definite target. We were on post #9. Corporal Mullinger came down to get a detail to go around and check the posts and see if anyone needed any help. We went to post #6 and picked up two wounded men and I stayed with them, while they went back. They brought more wounded men in and then the reinforcements got there. He went out to 106's. Two men were dead out there and two were alright. Lance Corporal L___Ly was left there with the 106. I saw just one V. C., and he was dead. We were very alert that night, because there was some fire in the daytime, and we were more or less expecting something to happen. He had just one grenade thrown at us, and some sniper fire. The grenade was thrown from behind us, from inside the perimeter.

WILLIAM T. DONAHUE
ENCL (22)

STATEMENT OF LANCE CORPORAL EUGENE J. HALL 2030113/0341 U.S. MARINE CORPS

13 November 1966

I, Lance Corporal Eugene J. Hall 2030113/0341 USMC, having been informed by Captain Leo J. KELLY of the matter under investigation and having first been advised of my rights under Article 31b of the Uniform Code of Military Justice do hereby voluntarily make the following statement:

I was in the 81's command post asleep when the attack commenced. I remember very little of the ensuing moments. I remember waking up when the explosions started. I was then shot twice and blacked out. The next thing I remember I was being helped to a medical facility. I have a faint recollection of Corporal Bothwell attempting to fire into the 81's ammo pit in an attempt to explode the rounds there in thus destroying the tube. I don't know where my weapon is.

EUGENE J. HALL

Lance Corporal Eugene J. Hall was located in C Med at the time this statement was made. He has since been evacuated out of the Republic of Vietnam. Certified to be a true statement of the above named.

L. J. KELLY
CAPT. USMC
ENCL (23)

Witnessed by

W. J. KANE, JR.
2nd Lt. USMC

STATEMENT OF LANCE CORPORAL THOMAS F. BANKS JUNIOR 2105033/0341, U.S. MARINE CORPS

12 November 1966

I, Lance Corporal Thomas F. Banks 2105033/0341 USMC, having been informed by Captain Leo J. Kelly of the matter under investigation and having first been advised of my rights under Article 31b of the Uniform Code of Military Justice do hereby voluntarily make the following statement: on the morning on 12 November 1966 I was on post 14, An Trach Village. I was posted on the north side of the perimeter. I stand guard duty approximately every three days. We split the watch up, it totals a six-hour watch apiece. Sometimes we stand it two hours on and two hours off. It differs from night. Some men like to work it 1800 to 2400 and others from 2400 to 0600. On this night we were a little nervous because of the round coming that day, we both stayed up until 2400. Everyone was nervous that night because we got hit that afternoon, we were hit pretty hard. So we were more or less expecting something to happen that night. At approximately 0700 on the 11th of November the Viet Cong opened up on us with small arms fire, I think there were some automatic weapons also. At 0130, 12 November 1966, we were sitting on the bunker when all hell broke loose. It sounded like they started dropping mortar rounds into the command post area. We didn't really know what was going on. We stayed in the bunker and then post 13 started yelling, we couldn't understand them. We were about 150 meters away from post 13. Post 14 is a bad post, there is a tree line within grenade range of the bunker, nobody likes to stand that post. Post 13 came over to our position; about this time the explosions in the back stopped. When they came over two were wounded, two grenades were thrown into their bunker from the rear of their position. A corporal was there, he took us back and set up a small 360 degree perimeter around the 81's tents to take care of the wounded. As far as I know the ARVN stayed on the perimeter. After we went to the 81's command post I do not think anyone even thought about the ARVN. There were some Viet Cong between us and post 1, but we couldn't open up on them because of the possible effect on post 1. We waited until they got in front of the perimeter and then opened up on them. The ARVN also opened up.

THOMAS F. BANKS
ENCL (24)

STATEMENT OF LANCE CORPORAL GEORGE E. JONSSON 2130292/0311, U.S. MARINE CORPS

12 November 1966

I, Lance Corporal George E. Jonsson 2130292/0311 USMC, having been informed by Captain Leo J. Kelly of the matter under investigation and having first been advised of my rights under Article 31b of the Uniform Code of Military Justice do hereby voluntarily make the following statement:

At 0100 hours 12 November I was on post 11, An Trach (1), on perimeter security. Private First Class Evans was on post with me. My watch started at 0040 hours. It was 0055 hours when the first explosion took place. I thought it was artillery at first, it sounded like it. I looked to my right and saw some more explosions. The whole command post area was hit. We were also receiving small arms fire from the front. We got back into the bunker and tried to contact the command post. The next thing that happened was explosions and rounds coming in on us from the rear. A corporal and some men came up from one of the other posts, the corporal had been shot in the leg. We went down to the tent and they decided to go out and get the wounded from the posts. We did everything we could and posted two men at post ten. After that we went down to the school. Corporal Ruiz was caught in the building; the ceiling had fell in on him. We took all the wounded back to the back to the 81's area. Then the reinforcements came.

GEORGE E. JONSSON
ENCL (25)

STATEMENT OF LANCE CORPORAL JAMES P. MOSELEY
2109668/0331, U.S. MARINE CORPS

12 November 1966

I, Lance Corporal James P. Moseley 2109668/0331 USMC, having been informed by Captain Leo J. Kelly of the matter under investigation and having first been advised of my rights under Article 31b of the Uniform Code of Military Justice do hereby voluntarily make the following statement:

On the morning of 12 November 1966, I had just got off watch at 033 hours. Corporal Meilinger relieved me. Then I heard explosions all over the place, mostly back to our left. I shot at some Viet Cong. I know that they were Viet Cong because they were in areas where no one was supposed to be. I do not know if I killed any of them. I did not know that we were going to be attacked that night.

JAMES P. MOSELEY
ENCL (26)

STATEMENT OF LANCE CORPORAL JOHN RAVENELL 215849/0351 U.S. MARINE CORPS

12 November 1966

I, Lance Corporal John Ravenell 2105849/0351 USMC, having been informed by Captain Leo J. Kelly of the matter under investigation and have first been advised of my rights under Article 31b of the Uniform Code of Military Justice do hereby make the following statement:

On the morning of 12 November 1966 at approximately 0100 hours I was on post as a sentry. I heard explosions from the other side of the perimeter. There was one other man on post with me, we were all awake at the time of the attack. We had just previously returned from an ambush positions near the crossroads and were still pretty keyed up. I had no idea there was going to be any attack on our position.

JOHN RAVENELL
ENCL (27)

STATEMENT OF PRIVATE FIRST CLASS GEORGE M.
KAUFFMAN 2246102/0311 U.S. MARINE CORPS

13 November 1966

I, Private First Class George M. Kauffman 2246102/0311 USMC,
having first been informed by Captain Leo J. Kelly of the matter
under investigation and having first advised of my rights under
Article 31b of the Uniform Code of Military Justice do hereby voluntarily make the following statement:

I was asleep when the first explosion occurred. I was thrown to the
deck when I tried to get up. I was hit with frequents in the head. I
was unconscious until the relief column came and rendered first aid.
They then took me to NSA. I don't know how the Viet Cong got
into our position.

GEORGE M. KAUFFMAN

Private First Class George M. Kauffman was located in C. Med at
the time this statement was made. He since has been evacuated out
of the Republic of Vietnam. Certified to be a true statement of the
above named individual.

L. J. KELLY
Captain USMC
ENCLO (28)

Witnessed by

W. J. KANE JR.
2nd Lt. USMC

STATEMENT OF PRIVATE FIRST CLASS ALEX HUGGINS JR, 224590/0311, U.S. MARINE CORPS

12 November 1966

I, Private First class Alex Huggins 2242509/0311 USMC, having been informed by Captain Leo J. Kelly of the matter under investigation and having first been advised of my rights under Article 31b of the Uniform Code of Military Justice do hereby voluntarily make the following statement:

I was on post #11, on the perimeter of An Trach at approximately 0100, 12 November 1966. I had just got off guard, and was trying to go to sleep when the incident took place. Corporal Meilinger went to the C. P. to see what happened, and got shot. I have an automatic rifle M-14, serial number 176670. I did not know that we were going to be attacked.

ALEX HUGGINS
ENCL (29)

STATEMENT OF PRIVATE FIRST CLASS NELSON L. JOHNSON 2243835/0311, U.S. MARINE CORPS

13 November 1966

I, Private First Class Nelson L. Johnson 2243825/0311 USMC having been informed by Captain Leo J. Kelly of the matter under investigation and having been first advised of my right under Article 31b of the Uniform Code of Military Justice do hereby make the following statement:

I was on post 6, in the school house with Lance Corporal Robinson, Corporal Hill and Private First Class Paulsen. Lance Corporal Robinson was on watch at the time of that attack. He yelled "attack" and called the other men to the post. We headed out of the house toward the command post. Explosions were coming from everywhere, I jumped into a hole. I saw the Viet Cong, dressed in black P. J.'s running in and out of the houses. I didn't know who they were. Then I heard Corporal Bryson yelling. The ARVNs and PATs would not move to help us. Then Corporal Bryson came and carried us to 81's command post where we were eventually taken to "C" Med.

NELSON L. JOHNSON

Private First Class Nelson L. Johnson was located in "C" Med at the time this statement was made. He has since been evacuated out of the Republic of Vietnam. Certified to be a true statement of the above named individual.

L. J. KELLY
Capt. USMC

Witnessed by

W. J. KANE JR.
2nd Lt. USMC

STATEMENT OF PRIVATE FIRST CLASS AUTHUR T. EVANS 2250235/0311, U.S. MARINE CORPS

12 November 1966

I, Private First Class Authur T. Evans 2250235/0311USMC, having been informed by Captain Leo J. Kelly of the matter under investigation and having first been informed of my rights under Article 31b of the Uniform Code of Military Justice do hereby voluntarily make the following statement.

At 0100 12 November 1966 I was on perimeter watch at post. Lance Corporal Johnson was on post at this time. He heard a few sniper rounds and came in and woke us up. Then mortars started coming in. A few minutes later, Corporal Meilinger came up to my post and we went to post #6 to see if there was anything left there. The only Viet Cong I saw were dead. I did not see any ARVN. The 81 mortars did not fire any concentrations as far as I know. I didn't hear any firing by the 81's all of the fire. 304008 is the number of my modified rifle. I didn't fire at all that night, nor did I have any idea that the command post was going to be hit.

AUTHUR T. EVANS
ENCL (31)

STATEMENET OF PRIVATE FIRST CLASS CARL G. BURGY
2229249/0311, U.S. MARINE CORPS

13 November 1966

I, Private First Class Carl G. Burgy 2229249/0311 USMC having been informed by Captain Leo J. Kelly of the matter under investigation and having first been advised of my rights under Article 31b of the Uniform Code of Military Justice do hereby voluntarily make the following:

I was posted on post 13 with Corporal Soccorso, Private First Class Wyatt and Private First Class Lance on the morning of the attached. I was on watch at the time of the attack. I heard automatic weapon fire and numerous explosions from inside the perimeter. Then someone came to our bunker and threw a grenade inside. We all jumped out. It didn't go off. We fired on the person who threw the grenade. We got back in the bunker and soon after another grenade was thrown in. The other men got out, I didn't make it. The grenade went off the next thing I remember I was in "C" Med.

CARL G. BURGY

Private First Class Carl g. Burgy 2229249/0311 was located in C Med at the time this statement was made. He was since been evacuated out of the Republic of Vietnam. Certified to be a true statement of the above named individual.

L. J. KELLY
Capt. USMC
ENCL (32)

Witnessed by

W. J. KANE JR.
2nd Lt. USMC

MARINE CORPS

12 November 1966

I Private First Class Douglas W. Whitfield 2232071/2532 USMC, having been informed by Captain Leo J. Kelly of the matter under investigation and having first been advised of my rights under Article 31b of the Uniform Code of Military Justice do hereby voluntarily make the following statement.

My job was that of the section radio operator, but at the time of the explosion I was sleeping in the rack. I would say that the attack took place about 0200, 12 November 1966. I was thrown out of the rock on the first explosion. After that all I heard was one explosion after another. We had a couple of rounds in the tent, and one was illumination, the other HE round. After the second or third round, the HE round went off. It threw me up in the air again, this is where I got my first shrapnel. After the explosions stopped, I heard someone outside the tent calling for 81's. He kept saying 81's, 81's. All of a sudden I heard a carbine shot, and then I heard a groan. So evidently whoever it was, got shot. I got up. Just as soon to see who was wounded. There was a man lying across the doorway. I crawled out the door and saw Gaughan laying in the road where the six comes through. He was covered to the shoulders with mud and water. I asked him if he wanted help, but he didn't answer. I tried to pick him up, and he started complaining about his leg, so I dragged him to the sand bags inside the bunker. I checked his pulse and it was alright. There wasn't anything that I could do for him, because I didn't know where he was hit or how bad he was hurt. I saw Bothwel as soon as I went out of the tent, and he was calling for 81's. I took him and laid him down where there was a clear area inside for the tent. The next thing I did was to go in and look for my weapons. I found my .45 pistol, and knew that there were still V. C. out there. I started wondering how we were going out to get out of this, so I started looking around for my radio. I looked over to my left and I saw the radio we use for radio watch. It was blown up. The battery casing was blown off, so I kept looking around and found another radio under my rack. Fortunately nothing had happened to it, so I put the whip antenna on it. One of the little kids, evidently wondering how we were, came into the tent. I turned on the radio, and asked him if he could hear anything. He said he could but all I could hear was jamming. Eventually I came up with the circumference Bailey frequency. I told them what the situation was. That we had wounded KIAs, and that we needed help, and that we might get hit again. Then I requested _____ Evac as soon as possible. I could hear circumference and chin strap conversing, but they couldn't hear me. I keep insisting that somebody do something because I didn't know what was going to happen next. All of a sudden Blackwell Bailey came out on the net, and as far as I can remember, they started putting artillery out there 500 or 600 meters out from our 81 positions. So I got a hold of Blackwell Bailey and they wanted assistance in calling in the artillery, and they started putting artillery out. Illumination was coming in and the canister started falling into the command post, so I told them to stop firing illumination. I then told them to go 150 meters right. At first they landed in 106's and they were not doing us any good. I was talking to Blackwell Bailey and they said that they were going to get us lied Evac. They called me and told that the choppers could not get to us because of the weather. I told him that the men were in serious condition and _____ that we _____ a Med evac immediately. I ask them if they could send vehicles of some sort, to get these people out. They said that medical support was on its way, with reinforcements. So we just sat around the tent waiting for something to happen. I was keeping communications with Chin, Strap, and Bailey. I kept calling and insisting that they send help immediately. Then the troops from the perimeter began coming in. We were glad to see them. They came in the tents, and I asked the senior ____ to keep the men quiet because they were making too much noise, and to have them clear the stuff away from the sand bags. He kept them quiet. Earlier an ARVN had come in from the road with his rifle over his shoulder like nothing had ever happened. He indicated to us that he was some kind of corpsman. The corporal had walked him down and told me to watch him. A little I saw the corporal and I told him that I couldn't watch him and keep communications at the same time. I went back to the radio. Circumference Bailey came up on the net and said reinforcements were on their way and they were about 2000 meters from our position. I requested that they fire a green cluster to let us know that they were out there, and they told me they would fire a white star cluster. So I told the guys to keep an eye to the South East. All of a sudden I heard 6-1. They were coming up on our frequency. I asked them for their position, and they said they were approximately 50 meters from the church. They fired a white star cluster right after they came over the bridge. All of a sudden I saw them coming down the road, and they came to our position and started helping us out. The six boys came right behind them, and they loaded them in the truck. I think they took us to regiment first, and took us off the six by and it looked like they put us in a chapel. They kept piling us in there. There was an ARVN on my right side and one on my left. A little later they evacuated us to Charlie med. I do not stand watch on the perimeter, but stand radio watch with the rest of the men. I don't know where the ARVN were during the attack. I knew they were ARVN because of the uniforms. I have no idea how the V. C. got inside the perimeter. We would have been previously notified of the oncoming attack, but as we were being hit, the perimeter was being hit too. We got hit early that morning, it seemed that two mortar rounds were fired at us. One hit on each side of the C. P. From what I figured, they were bracketing for an upcoming mortar attack, and all they would have had to done was put a round right between the other two, and they would have gotten everybody. They poured gas on the ammo and it exploded. All I could see was a black spot, moving away from the 81 position. As far as I know, they have my pistol at regiment. My pistol # is 1996159.

DOUGLAS W. WHITFIELD

STATEMENT OF PRIVATE FIRST CLASS
NORMAN T. WYATT 2267088/0311, U.S. MARINE CORPS

12 November 1966

I, Private First Class Norman T. Wyatt 2267088/0311 USMC, having been informed by Captain Leo J. Kelly of the matter under investigation and having first been advised of my rights under Article 31b do hereby make the following statement:

On 12 November 1966, I was on post #13 at about 0030, I was lying down to go to sleep. I heard about three shots coming from our forward tree line. I got up and heard something make a noise behind us. A Vietnamese ran up to the bunker, and was pulling a pin on a grenade. He put his hand on the bunker and threw it in. I grabbed my rifle and jumped out and shot at him. We got back into the bunker and another grenade came flying in. We all jumped out and sat in front of our bunker about five minutes later we heard explosion soon, and I guess about four perimeter, and carbine rounds coming from the outside of the perimeter. We figured they had taken over the perimeter. We went down to post #14 and picked up the two marines on that post. We decided to go back to the C. P. area. My rifle # is 117176. I did not know there was going to be an attack. We were hit pretty hard in the morning. I don't think that 81's fired any concentrations that night.

NORMAN T. WYATT
ENCL (34)

STATEMENT OF PRIVATE FIRST CLASS JOSEPH E. DYKES
2055052/0341 U.S. MARINES CORPS

12 November 1966

I, Private First Class Joesph E. Dykes 2055052/0341 USMV, Having been informed by Captain Leo J. Kelly of the matter under investigation and having first been advised of my rights under Article 31b or the Uniform Code of Military Justice do hereby voluntarily make the following statement.

On 12 November 1966 about 0100 I was sleeping. I had just got off watch at 0001. During the day we had some incoming rounds. About 0100 or so the man on post #10 that was on watch came and woke me up. I heard an explosion, and thought it was mortar rounds coming in. I went into the bunker and got my rifle. All of us went into the bunker. After the explosions stopped I climbed out of the bunker and grenade landed between us and post # 11. My rifle # is 4484640. I had no idea that they were going to attack us.

JOSEPH E. DYKE
ENCL (35)

STATEMENT OF PRIVATE FIRST CLASS JERRY E. BROWN
2260762/0311 U.S. MARINE CORPS

12 November 1966

I, Private First Class Jerry E. Brown 2260762/0311 USMC, having been informed by Captain Leo J. Kelly of the matter under investigation and having first been advised of my rights under Article 31b of the Uniform Code of Military Justice do hereby voluntarily make the following statement.

I had just come in off ambush and had manned post #8. I had just dozed off to sleep, and PFC Mcnell woke myself and Lance Corporal Lance up. I did not see any Viet Cong. I did not know we were going to be attacked

JERRY E. BROWN
ENCL (36)

STATEMENT OF PRIVATE FIRST CLASS DAVID E. LAMBERT
2269648/0351. U.S. MARINE CORPS

12 November 1966

I, Private First Class David E. Lambert 226948/0351 USMC, having
been informed by Captain Leo J. Kelly of the matter under investigation and having first been advised of my rights under Article 31b
of the Uniform Code of Military Justice do hereby voluntarily make
the following statement:

Right before the attack I was sleeping. The only unusual occurrence
that night was a dog barking, this dog usually doesn't bark at anything at all, but apparently it was never investigated. The barking
came from behind us about 50 yards away. Over near the church
right between the church and the mess hall was where I heard the
barking come from. The barking occurred about 0015 hours, I had
just got off watch and was getting ready to hit the rack. I think it was
someone inside the perimeter because the dog only barked two or
three times. If it had been someone outside the perimeter he would
have barked continuously. The first grenade landed right beside my
rack on the outside of the bunker. Jimmy was in the couch when the
grenade went off, I do not know where he went. Corporal Ayala and
Defilippis were getting out too. I thought it was incoming mortar
rounds at first, they hit us so fast. I would sat at least five grenades
went off at our tent alone. I went out to the 106 and took my position as A-Gunner, waiting for something to happen. Then Defilippis
got hit. We couldn't see any flashes. We weren't sure where the shot
came from, but it was from back of us. Ayala went to see if Mamasan
would help Defilippis. Then we were hit again. I saw a grenade go
off right next to PFC Boyette. I thought for sure he was dead. From
the 106 position I saw three V. C. running across the field. I fired at
them, but didn't hit any of them. It looked like they were carrying
magazines they had taken from us, but I am not sure. I don't think
Ayala had a weapon with him when he was hit, unless the V. C.
took it. The C. P. got his exactly the same time we got hit. This was

about 0100. I think the ARVN went back to his position which is 50 meters to our left rear. Post #3. I believe that there are four ARVN at that post. I never heard a round from the ARVN in that post all the time during before or after the attack. We can't keep contact with this post, we cannot communicate with the Vietnamese, for the language barrier. There are no PATS around at all. I didn't leave my position until approximately 0800 that morning.

DAVID E. LAMBERT
ENCL (37)

STATEMENT OF PRIVATE FIRST CLASS DAVID F. JOHNSON 2216662/0331, U.S. MARINE CORPS

12 November 1966

I, Private First Class David F. Johnson 2216662/0331, USMC, having been informed by Captain Leo J. Kelly of the matter under investigation and having first been advised of my rights under Article 31b of the Uniform Code of Military Justice do hereby voluntarily make the following statement:

At approximately 0100 on 12 November 1966, I had just came back from patrol and went to post 12. I heard an explosion, I turned around and saw a couple more explosions. There were some carbine rounds coming in around post 12. We did not fire on them we just waited. On post 13 to our right, we heard rounds going off and an explosion. Corporal Soccorso was over there. On our way over to post 13 we saw a Viet Cong threw a grenade into post 13. The Viet Cong opened up on them. The Viet Cong hit Corporal Meilinger on the hip. Lance Corporal Kimmey shot the Viet Cong. Then they went over to 13 and then came back to post 12. The gunner and I then went to post 12 and stayed we had no communication with the command post. We tried to get the command post on the phone but no one answered, when we got back to the command post 81's were knocked out. There were some dead men lying all over. So we took our team and went down to posts 11, 10, 9 and 8, they were the only positions that weren't hit. There wasn't much left of the 81's command post, dead men lying all over. We set up a 360 degree perimeter round the Command Post then just set there and waited for help. I didn't see any ARVN until after daylight came. They were running around picking up everything. I took an M-14 away from one of them, he had a cartridge belt also. They were picking up any gear that they could get hold of. The only Viet Cong I saw was by the church, he was dead, we heard noises in the tree lines, we fired 15 rounds twice. The attack was completely by surprise.

DAVID F. JOHNSON
ENCL (38)

STATEMENT OF PRIVATE FIRST CLASS JAMES M. DAKE 2191554/0341, U.S. MARINE CORPS

12 November 1966

I, Private First Class James M. Dake 2191554/0341 USMC, having been informed by Captain Leo J. Kelly of the matter under investigation and having first been advised of my rights under Article 31b of the Uniform Code of Military Justice do hereby voluntarily make the following statement:

On 12 November 1966, at approximately 0130, I was on post 14 with Lance Corporal Banks. We usually have one marine and one ARVN that alternate every two or three hours. We had received a lot of incoming fire the day before, so Lance Corporal Banks and myself both were a little nervous that night so we decided to stand a 100% watch. I know there were two ARVN to our rear and slightly to our right near the bunker. We kept asking them if they were ARVN and they kept answering "yes." Then about one half hour later we heard an explosion from post 13, we heard someone yell, "We've been hit." We then heard some splashing to our right, it sounded like someone running away from the perimeter. We couldn't shoot because of the location of post 1. The ARVN cut loose as soon as the Viet Cong got out to where they could be shot at safely. Post 13 came down to our position and said that they had lost contact with post 12. Then a man came up to the post and told us that the Viet Cong broke into the command post and that they were trying to set up another perimeter. We went back to the command post. Mainly what we did was bandage the wounded, then we formed a 360 around the 81's tents. The ARVN remained on post all this time as far as we know. We gave them instructions to stay there. Post 14 was located at the northwest corner of the perimeter. I did not see any Viet Cong except for the one that escaped from the perimeter.

JAMES M. DAKE
ENCL (39)

STATEMENT OF PRIVATE FIRST CLASS PAUL A. MCNEIL 2280209/0311, U.S. MARINE CORPS

12 November 1966

I, Private First Class Paul R. Mcnein 2280209/0311, having been informed by Captain J. Kelly of the matter under investigation and having first been advised of my rights under Article 31b of the Uniform Code of Military Justice do hereby voluntarily make the following statement:

At approximately 0100, 12 November 1966 I was on watch at post 8. At the time we had a 75 percent watch, we had just came back from patrol about 0300 hours. Most of the time there are two asleep on watch and one awake. I heard a sound like it was mortars coming out of the tube. When the mortars hit we received some sniper rounds from our right front, when we heard explosions and people screaming. I fired my weapon at sniper rounds that were coming in. We tried to get the command post on the phone but I guess they were already wiped out. Corporal Meilinger came up and looked over what we had left. We went to the command post and set up a perimeter. The ARVN were manning their posts. They got hit the same time post 6 did. There is about 100 meters between post 6 and 7. I did not see any ARVN on post 7.

PAUL R. MCNEIL
ENCL (40)

STATEMENT OF PRIVATE FIRST CLASS DALLAS R. LAY 2152146/0311, U.S. MARINE CORPS

12 November 1966

I, Private First Class Dallas R. Lay 2152416/0311 USMC, having been informed by Captain Leo J. Kelly of the matter under investigation and having first been advised of my rights under Article 31b of the Uniform Code of Military Justice do hereby voluntarily make the following statement:

At 0300 hours on 12 November 1966 I got off watch on post 13. At about 0045 I laid down and started to go asleep, when a Viet Cong grenade was thrown in the bunker causing everybody to scramble outside. When we got back in a Viet Cong sprayed the top of the bunker with a grease gun, then threw in a charge, everybody got out except one man, he received a concussion as a result of it. There was fire coming from a free line in back of our bunker, so we moved into the ride paddy in front of the bunker. I saw one Viet Cong. On the second shot that I shot at him my rifle blew up in my face. I then went to post 14 and got an M-1 off one of the ARVN. Then we started for the command post, which was all in shambles when we got there. There were men laying all over the place, so we started patching them up. The only ARVN I saw were the ones manning post 14 and one in the command post helping aid the men. No ARVN could be seen. My rifle number is 1161144. I switched rifles with the ARVN, and at present I do not know where it is. It was an automatic weapon.

DALLAS R. LAY
ENCL (41)

STATEMENT OF LANCE CORPORAL LARRY A. KIMMY 2154493/0331, U.S. MARINE CORPS

12 November 1966

I, Lance Corporal Larry A. Kimmy 2154493/0331 USMC, having been informed by Captain Leo J. Kelly of the matter under investigation and having first been advised of my rights under Article 31b of the Uniform Code of Military Justice do hereby voluntarily make the following statement:

Myself and Private First Class Johnson had just got off patrol, we went to relieve post 9; upon our return at approximately 0100 I laid down. Corporal Meilinger was on watch. I heard something that sounded like mortars. Right away we tried to call the command post but we couldn't get any contact. As we started toward the command post, post 13 called. As we were going toward post 13 someone called out—"Watch out." We thought we heard some moving. Corporal Meilinger yelled out, "Who's there." Before we knew it a Viet Cong opened up with an automatic and hit Meilinger—Meilinger flipped over. I shot the Viet Cong several times. On the way back we ran into a trough of water and I lost my rifle and my helmet. From there we went back to the mortar men who were lying everywhere. We made a hasty defense while the corporals held a conference. They were trying to decide between two alternatives, (1) to get every available man back to regiments, or (2) to set up a hasty defense at the 81's command post. They decided to set up a defense. We then went down to bunkers 10, 9 and 8, then had men in them. None of the bunkers from 7 on were hit. We went to post 6 and it was in shambles. Corporal Ruiz was there and he was hit either in the back or chest, I do not know which. Another guy was shot in the leg, I believe his name was Johnson. We left two men in post 8, 9, 10 and 11, with specific order to watch every direction. When it was all over the ARVN started coming out. In the morning Johnson thought that we were being mortared, because whatever was exploding big, real big! Until 2200 hours we have a 100 percent watch. From 2200 hours on we have one man awake the rest asleep. We had three men awake at that time because we just returned from a patrol. I saw one Viet Cong besides the one I shot he was strangled by the cook. When we returned the one Viet Cong I shot was not there.

LARRY A. KIMMY
ENCL (42)

STATEMENT OF PRIVATE FIRST CLASS GARY R. BOYETT
2069071/0351, U.S. MARINE CORPS

12 November 1966

I, Private First Class Gary R. Boyett 2069071/0351 USMC, having
been informed by Captain Leo J. Kelly of the matter under investigation and having first been advised of my rights under Article 31b
of the Uniform Code of Military Justice do hereby voluntarily make
the following statement:

I was standing guard at the 106's position, post 2. I really didn't
see much of anything. At the time of the attack I was sitting at the
machine gun bunker watching the front of the perimeter. When
the first grenade went off I thought it was an artillery round. The
first grenade went off inside our sleeping quarters, no one was hurt.
Myself and the A-Gunner went immediately to the 106, our squad
leader was supposed to go to the gun but he stayed with the machine
gun. The Viet Cong opened up on me with an automatic weapon, I
dove for a ditch, I yelled back that I wasn't hit, the Viet Cong threw
another grenade at me it landed about three feet from me, I was
still alright, after they threw the next grenade at me I didn't make
any more noise just laid still. That is where I stayed the rest of the
night. I didn't see any Viet Cong at all. Corporal Ayala was trying
to get someone to help Defilippis when he was shot. I ran back and
could not find my weapon, there was nothing else for me to do buy
lay in the ditch. They fired at Defilippis in the machine gun bunker
with an automatic weapon. Then I heard the rattling of two rifles,
they were putting them on their shoulders. I know that they came
from our position. I cannot honestly say how they got into position.
ARVN fire from their post, during and after the attack I do not know
what happened to them. There are no marines at post 3, just ARVN.
It was very dark and our posts wore too far apart, so it wasn't very
hard for them to infiltrate our lines. We had no illumination whatso-
ever. I did not know there was going to be an attack. I do not think
anyone, not even the villager knew about the attack. I gave my rifle

to Sergeant Maiva. 13606073 is my M-14 rifle number. Vietnamese civilians lived inside the perimeter. We had a Vietnamese boy sleeping in our quarters that night, it is my personal opinion that Viet Cong came in and got the boy before they threw the grenades. His name was Jimmy, he had only one eye.

GARY R. BOYETT
ENCL (43)

LJK/jwm
5800
1 Dec 196

That listening posts be used extensively around all defensive positions.

That any marine unit that have ARVN soldiers or PATs co-loc with it be authorized to have the senior marine officer present be responsible for all defensive positions, and have the authority to place ARVN troops and PATs positions, and have the authority to place ARVN troops and PATs in the perimeter as needed.

L. J. KELLY

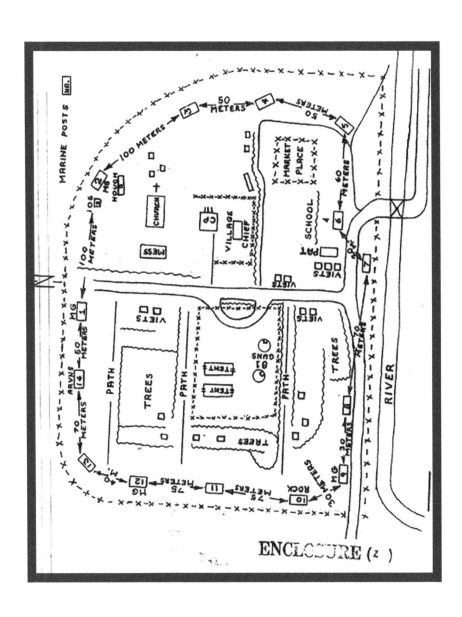

ENCLOSURE (2)

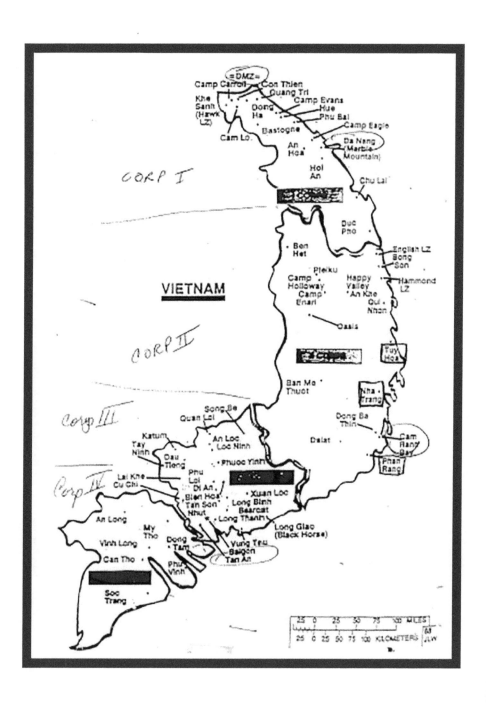

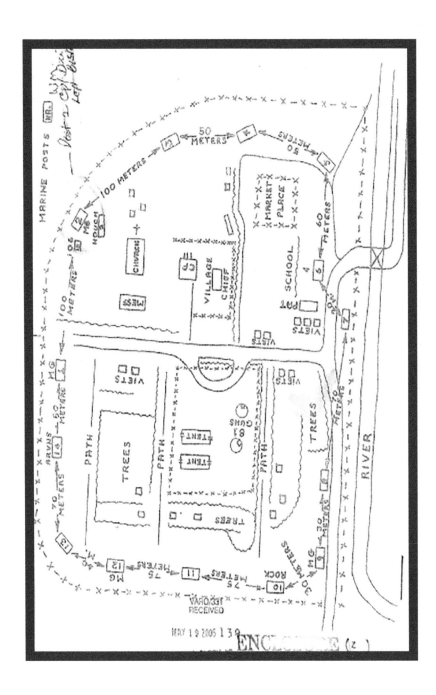

CHAPTER 24

I could see lights and hear people talking and not knowing where I waa. A very sad sign for me. I took the pen and signed my name. I was rolled off in a hurry into a room with bright lights. I could hear people talking in medical terminology.

I opened my eyes, and I could see this beautiful blue sky, and the sea touched the sky. It was quiet, and it was beautiful. I remembered what had happened to me. I thought I was in heaven. I thought I had died. I tried to get up to walk. I looked around and noticed the hospital bed and bandage on my stomach. A male nurse came to me and said it was good I was awake. Then other medical nurse and doctors came to my bedside. The doctor said, "You know you are a very important marine. General Westmorland slept in that chair last night, waiting to talk to you about what happened." As he told me it was necessary to keep me from getting pneumonia, the doctor made me swallow a plastic tube. I'm in the army hospital in the Philippines. The nurse would give me a shot every four hours that would make me feel good, and then I would go to sleep. As the days passed, they eventually made me get up and walk. I was up walking, getting my strength back. I started asking for the shot for pain. The nurse told me I was not going to get any more shots because I would be addicted to the drug. I got a haircut. I hadn't had my hair cut in two months.

The chaplain came to talk to me, and he informed me that Gary Newton from my unit was in the same hospital. I was glad to hear that. I found out where he was, and I went to see him. He was in a sweat and in pain. He looked at me and extended his hand. He gripped my hand, and tears came from his eyes. He told me they had cut his leg off. He was afraid his girlfriend wouldn't want a man with one leg. I told him that he would be standing tall when she saw him, and he shouldn't worry about that now. I told him we were the lucky ones because we got out alive. I promised to come back to visit the next day. The next day I was med-evaced to Guam, U.S. naval hospital in the Marina Islands.

Guam is where you would be patched up to go back to Vietnam or to the USA. The wounds I received from that grenade hit me in the eye, arms, stomach, chest, and both legs. I was able to call my wife, Betty, from Guam.

Women's Group Fetes Veterans—Nearly thirty veterans of Vietnam were guests of honor at a Guamanian-style dinner and entertainment on February 26, given at the Agana Heights residence of Senator and Mrs. George M. Bamba. The dinner was sponsored by the Agana Heights Women's Group. The dinner, the third one held, was an annual project of the ladies' group. The men were recuperating here before returning to duty in Vietnam. (Journal photo by Alvarez)

The letters began to come to me from my company in Da Nang. When I would lie in bed, I would think about what happened to I Company at Antrack. I got scared thinking about it. It was like a dream that would come every night before I would go to sleep.

A priest came to the hospital to see me. He told me that there were about 150 marines killed at Antrack. I asked about Danny Polison, Yarnell, Powell. He told me that they were all dead. He said Powell's position took a direct hit, and there were fewer marines in the bunker with Sergeant Powell. That made me real sad. Powell was a good marine to get killed like that. He will always be in my memory. I planned to find his family in Kansas City.

Life in Guam was okay. I met many marines, navy, and army personnel while there. The marines had a liaison office in the hospital to help the wounded get their paperwork and notification to relatives. Sergeant Harris was the NCOIC at the hospital office. Sergeant Harris would let me use the typewriter to send letters home. Since I could type, I would help them type orders up and do office work while recuperating.

I became friends with Sergeant Price, who worked at the liaison office. He had four months before he left Guam. Price told Sergeant Harris that he should consider me as his replacement since I had nine months left overseas. Either I would go back to Vietnam or serve nine months somewhere back in the bush. Sergeant Price lived in town with a Guam woman whom he had a child with. I went home with Price many times, but he told me not to tell the woman he was going back to the States. I stopped going home with him after I listened to her planning on going back to the United States with Price.

This was not going to happen. She had a small car and would come to the hospital to pick Price up. I could see this blowing up on me. Price was sick. When he left, she would be crying on my shoulder and getting angry with me about him. Sergeant Harris didn't like the woman. When she would come to the hospital, Harris wouldn't let her come into the office. Price would go outside with her most of the time, and she would leave mad. I found out she wanted Price to marry her. She didn't know he was married already.

President Johnson came to the hospital to award the Purple Heart to the veterans. I received the medal and was very proud to meet the president of the United States. The next week, General Wallace M. Green Jr., the commandant of the marine corps awarded me my second Purple Heart.

I was healing and feeling better. I was keeping up with the time I had left to serve overseas. It was now January 1967. I went to Vietnam in July 1966. I had just six more months. Sergeant Harris got me assigned to the marine barracks on Guam, and I was detached to the marine's liaison office at the hospital. My quarters were on the hospital grounds. Harris was to leave in about two weeks, so he showed me the job and my living quarters. The liaison team would meet the medivac each week at the airport. We would process all the paperwork for those who were wounded and would stay at Guam. I learned a lot at the office, and I enjoyed my job because there was no marching or formation to attend. I went to work at 0800 and got off at 1700, unless an airplane was coming in with wounded men.

Price slowly moved his belongings to the barracks, and he was gone in three days. I had not seen his girlfriend in a month. She came to the hospital and asked about Sergeant Harris. I just kept typing with my head down. Sergeant Harris went out in the hall to talk with her. I heard something about an emergency leave, and he would be back. He told her to get out of the office. That was the last time I saw her.

CHAPTER 25

After thirty years, Sergeant Harris was to retire. He was replaced by a new NCOIC, Rogers. He was slow and not too smart. I don't know where they got him from. The next week we got to Sergeant Lawler, and these two marines didn't like each other. Both were sergeants, but Rogers was in charge. Lawler told me I had some R&R coming, so did he. He suggested that we island hop to Saipan and Tinnion Islands. That Friday, we went to the airport and got on a small twin-engine airplane, and we took off to Saipan. The island was very small. We did the tour and stayed at a small hotel that was run by retired Americans. The next day, we went to Turtle Island, where the economy was based on turtle meat and shells. I enjoyed the trip. It was just a getaway. We had plenty of whiskey and beer but no women.

Two months passed, and now I'm thinking about going home. I had only four more months. All my letters to Betty had to do with going back. Two weeks later, I went to the office, and I was told to go to the marine barrack on Signal Hill. When I went to the office, the captain informed me that he was cutting me orders to go back to the United States because my sister was dying in St. Louis. I needed to be with my mother. The captain told me I would have to come back to Guam. He said, "You leave at 1500. Good luck." I went back to the office and said good-bye. I got my seabag and was carried to the airport. I boarded a Pan American 707, and I went to sleep.

I was awakened by the playing of the "Star-Spangled Banner," because the plane was going across the international time zone. We were leaving out darkness into the daytime. I looked back and could see night and looked forward and could see the sun shining. I landed in San Francisco on a military base. I got a cab to the regular airport. I was unaware that an airline strike was in process, and flights were limited. I had to wait around for hours before I got a flight to Washington, DC, to connect to St. Louis. I was put on a flight in Piedmont Airlines. It was a prop with two engines. That airplane stopped three times before I got to Washington, DC. It was Sunday morning, and I was standing against the wall at the airport, waiting for my flight home. All of a sudden, a short man with a big white hat was standing directly in front of me. He was looking me in the eye, saying, "Son, you have been fighting, but you don't know why. My name is Martin Luther King Jr. God bless you, son." I said thanks and shook his hand, and he and four big black men walked away. I had just met Martin Luther King Jr. His words are with me today.

I left DC and arrived in St. Louis Sunday afternoon. As I walked off the plane down the steps, I got down on my knees and kissed the pavement. The people looked at me, and I said out loud, "This is a long way from Vietnam. I'm glad to be home." I got my seabag and walked to the exit, and I saw John Warren, who was also in his army uniform. John said his father was picking him up and they would take me home. John and I talked, and his father was glad to see me. They took me to Betty's mother's house at 4915 Farlin. I didn't have time to call Betty. She didn't know I was coming because she and Obine didn't get along at all.

I knocked on the door, and Lillie Ward opened the door. As she called Betty, she said, "Willie is here." Betty looked at me like I was a ghost. We kissed, and I greeted her parents and told them I was tired. Betty had her bags packed because she was going to New York the next day to visit her friends. The trip was cancelled. I told her, "I'm back. I have only two months left to serve." I called my mother, and she came to take me to the hospital to see my sister. Josie got better, and she was discharged. I had only five days' leave before I had to go to Camp Lejeune, North Carolina. The days passed quickly, and I visited my father on the farm. Before I knew it, time was up.

CHAPTER 26

I left St. Louis to report to Camp Lejeune. I felt good because I knew it wouldn't be long before I would be discharged. I was given orders to go to Guantanomo, Cuba, for the rest of my time. We boarded the ship with full gear. I didn't know much about what the marine corps was doing down there. I would find out very soon. The ship was a troop transport. My group was down in the belly of the ship. The racks for sleeping were very close. There was just enough room for you to slide in, which was about fifteen inches above and below your body. When we got underway, some of the marines got seasick. They were throwing up all over the ship and hanging over the side. It was going to take us four days to cruise to Cuba. I stayed down in the rack most of the time until it was time to eat.

Most of us didn't eat the first days because the ship was in rough waters, and it tossed from side to side and up and down. Food was the last thing you wanted. I ate crackers, and it didn't affect me much. I taught some of the marines how to play Tonk, a card game. We played until we got to Cuba. I had won money, and this trip was over.

I met Reginald Lindsey and Newburn while stationed in Cuba. Lindsey was from Kansas City, and Newburn was from Chicago. Lindsey was short and getting out soon. Everyone in my group was short and getting out soon. Cuba was hot, and the insects were big. I never saw flies so big. The climate reminded me of Vietnam. Lindsey and I became friends. We hung together, and I had the rank. Lindsey said he had been busted for fighting a sergeant while in Vietnam. He said he just wanted to get out and back to his job at General Motors.

The time passed in Cuba slowly. We would have to go on red alerts and man the lines when Cubans would try to cross the border. This drill would go on four or five times a week. This was like a staging unit for marines. We didn't have much to do. It was either guard duty or cleaning up or loading trucks. Most of the time we played cards, shot dice, or played records. We tried to stay out of trouble. We were loose, too loose.

A week before it was time to go back to Camp Lejeune, they let us buy whiskey. It was duty-free, and we stored it on the ship. Foster and Joe were loading the whiskey and got their hands on the quarts of 151 rum and brought it back to the barracks. Everyone close to us got a taste. The marines and whiskey didn't mix. It was trouble. We had been there in Cuba for five weeks and went on liberty for about five hours in the town. There was nothing there worthwhile. There were a few restaurants and an NCO club full of Cuban fags. Lindsey and I went back. Joe, Newburn, and Foster had gotten drunk on 151 Run.

It was time to turn the lights out in the barracks and quiet down. I got a drink and lay down to sleep. The MP came and told the group to cut the lights and stand down. As soon as the MPs left, they turned up the music and kept partying. Lindsey lay down and made jokes about them getting locked up because no whiskey was allowed on the base.

I was in the rack, and here come the MPs with their .45s out, and they got Foster, Newburn, and Jamaica Joe. They took them to the brig. Cuba had a redline jail, which meant that they beat your ass. It was the worst place to be incarcerated. The next day, we saw Foster and Joe on a garbage truck with their covers on backward and in prison uniform. They couldn't look up. The guard told them to look down and they didn't deserve to look at the sky. Lindsey said, "It's hell to pay the captain. They might be down here for a year."

The baseball season was in, and I started a home run pool. Whoever picked the baseball player with the most home runs in a week would win the cash. I took my cut for running the pool. Lindsey called me Popeye, and I called him the Glip. The captain had found out our group was where the whiskey was stolen and brought in.

They had a search of the barracks and found my baseball stuff. The next day at formation, the captain asked "Who is Popeye?" and no one said anything. I said, "Popeye, I, I, sir." He asked, "Can I get into the baseball pool?" I answered, "No, sir. The pool is closed down due to Foster's arrest." The captain didn't say anything else and stopped the pool because they weren't going to lock me up for gaming on U.S. government property. They let Newburn and Forster out of jail, and they joined us for the return to North Carolina.

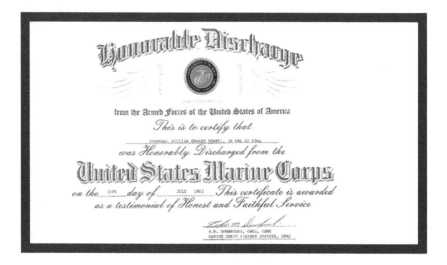

When I got back, I had to report to the recruiting officer. He tried to tell me I had a great future with the marine corps and I should sign up for four more years. I would get a stripe and a cash bonus. I told him, "No, thanks, I'm going home." He gave me my papers and flight papers. On the way out of his office, Ronald Jones was coming in to talk to the recruiting officer. I waited for Ronald to come out. He didn't stay in there long either.

Ronald told me had been in the hospital, and I told him I just returned from Cuba. He said he was going home in another week. I was ready to go home the next day, and the *Pueblo* incident happened with China, and all order were frozen. The *Pueblo* was a ship, and whatever happened, I couldn't go home. They kept me there for a week. It was explained that I was part of the ready reserve unit, and I had to wait until Washington gave the okay to let me go home.

CHAPTER 27

I was out and on my way home. I got a cab and called Betty to tell her that I was on my way to the house. Everyone was happy to see me. Betty worked at Southwestern Bell Telephone Company, and it was Saturday when I got home. On Sunday, her parents went to church. I told Betty that I wanted to go to the bank. I needed money to buy clothes. Most of my old clothes were at my mother's house in East Boogie. Obine had left Mr. Russell. She lived with my brother Donald on Sixty-Eighth Street. I called Obine and told her I wanted my red convertible Chevy. It was in the garage at the tavern. Obine drove over to Betty's and picked me up. We talked, and Obine complained that Betty had done her wrong since I had been in the service. When we got to the garage, Obine said, "Now don't get upset. There has been an accident with your car." I looked at her and asked who wrecked my car. I opened the garage, and my car had been hit head-on. The whole front end was folded up like a train had hit. I asked her who did it. Obine said that Babyboy, my cousin, did it. I asked how he got his hands on my car. Obine didn't say anything else. She said that Russell was going to get it fixed. The truth came out later, and the deal was Obine was renting my car to Olive Ezell, "Babyboy," because he didn't have a car. He got drunk and had some bitch driving my car, and she hit the back of a truck in St. Louis.

Obine took me back home, and I was mad. I couldn't really be mad at Babyboy because Obine rented the car out. That put a wedge between us. Coming back, Obine complained that Betty wasn't any good because she kept her from getting some heating oil. Obine used Betty's name and job to get fuel to heat the house. The oil company contacted Betty at work, and Betty stopped that oil shipment. I don't know what was said, but my mother had her slick side on, doing things to get what she needed. Obine and Betty never got along.

I called on Black Sunday and asked Betty for money. She didn't have a dime. She was supposed to be saving the bonds she got twice a month from my pay. I wanted to have money from that when I got out. Obine didn't have my clothes. She probably gave them away or sold them. I had nice clothes when I went in the marines. All I saw was one pair of shoes. I was back home with no money, no clothes, and little food.

Betty and I had to sleep in the basement on a rollaway bed. I lay in the bed, thinking I had been gone for two years and things weren't right. When Betty got up to go to work, I had her drop me off at the packinghouse. I reported back to work. I was out of the service on Saturday and at work on Monday. I got my same old job back, and the fellows were glad to see me. Ralph Harris was still cutting meat where I left him years ago. The white boy who couldn't read a scale or weigh meat was there wearing a white frock with Superintendent's Office written on it. Before I went to service, this man could hardly count. He was a dropout. He never finished high school. I asked him how he landed that job. He told me they had a course of study if you got sponsored by the Swift Company. I went to the company and asked if I could get in the program. They told me that they would get back with me. Later that month, I reminded them that I was still interested in the program. Mr. Bondy, the personnel manager, called me to the office and informed me that program was closed. It wasn't offered anymore. I knew what had happened. He knew I would be trouble. So if there was no program, I couldn't hold anyone responsible.

The next week, I was moved to the night shift in the aged beef department. This was my punishment; if I wanted to get paid, I would work wherever I was told. I talked to Ralph Harris about it, and he said to forget it. Ralph had gotten married, and he was there for the duration. I was moved to a new job every week. After two weeks, I went on vacation with pay. Ralph told me I had it coming when I went to the marines. I really needed that two-week vacation money because I couldn't stand sleeping in that musty basement.

When Betty's parents went to the meat market, Mrs. Ward would write her name on the package. That meant that it was her meat. When that happened, I knew I had to get my own real quick. The vacation money and time took care of that problem. I was on the bus going on West Florissant and noticed an apartment building with a For Rent sign in the window. I went to the apartment. A white lady was there, painting the walls. I asked if the apartment was still for rent, and she said yes. I told her my sad story about the military and how I was living in my in-laws' basement. She asked where I worked. I proudly told her about Independent Packing Company on Chouteau Avenue. She gave me an application and told me to bring it back. I filled it out right there. The woman was very nice. She was the manager.

After she looked over the application, she asked when I wanted to move in. I told her "Right away." She told me it would be a week before the apartment would be painted and finished. I told her that I would finish the painting myself. She told me I could have the apartment and could move in. I gave her $160. The rent was $80 a month. The apartment was nice, with four rooms and all hardwood floors.

When Betty got home from work, I took her to the place, and she was pleased. Betty said she would get the furniture we needed on credit from Greenburg Furniture Store on Delmar. I didn't care. I had my own place now. We settled in and had our love nest. We got a car, and things were going great. Betty got pregnant with my first girl. June Elizabeth Dowell was born December 4, 1969.

Obine didn't communicate much because things were going okay for me. I would call, but the conversation was always pertaining to money. Obine was with Glen Little and working at a grocery store. She was having a hard time because Glen was like a pimp. He had no job, but he liked to gamble. If Obine had money, Glen had money. Obine eventually went back to live with Russell after Glen tricked her.

28

I was rolling good now. I had my family, a car, and a job. Now I had to go back to school. The VA gave me the money and a check each month for going to college.

I went back to the junior college at Forest Park. I was focused. I took sixteen hours of study and finally graduated the following May. It was the school's first commencement at Forest Park. I was proud, and I had to keep education first. I remembered how I was treated at the packinghouse. That program didn't exist for me, but it did for the white men.

I enrolled at St. Louis University. This had been my dream when I was in high school. John Smith had played basketball for St. Louis University. I was in arts and sciences and business administration. Even though the work was hard, I remembered being in Vietnam. I could do anything. I would not be denied anything I set a goal to do. The only problem I had was a statistics class. The professor told me to go to his office. He was a marine, and he knew I was having a hard time with the course. He said I didn't have to attend class. He told me to read one chapter a week and meet him on Fridays for an oral exam. This worked well. Then the supervisor at the packinghouse found out I was going to college. "You make $3.75 an hour. They care about the cows." I heard him again and he actually told me, "If you like the money, keep doing the work. If not, leave."

Each week I would go job hunting because I didn't have to be at work until 1:00 p.m. One day I stopped down to Hi Wells to get a tripe and sandwich, and I went across the street to get a beer at the tavern. Hawaitha, "Hide," was there getting ready to open the tavern.

He got me a drink, and we talked. He was glad to see me. He told me that they went and visited Obine on Sundays. They ate and talked about old times. I told Hide I was not satisfied with my job. The money was good, but the work was hard, and it was cold in there. Hide told me that Conrad Liquor Company was hiring salesmen. He gave me the address and the phone number. He said, "Baby brother, they make good money. I said I would call them.

I went to work the following day, and after a few hours working in that cold room, my nose and ears began bleeding. I went to the nurse's office for help. The doctor looked inside my ear and told me to go to the hospital. I went to the VA on Grand. I was admitted. The doctor had told me he was going to operate immediately. I called Betty, and she came to the hospital where they had done the operation, and I was sick when I woke up. I stayed in the VA for a week. I had sick leave from the plant, so I still got paid.

Obine came to the hospital, and so did Willie. He was still working in the hid cellar at the plant. My grandfather James Coleman was working at the plant as the sewer man, keeping the lines open. Three generations in the plant—the sewer, the cellar, and the beef floor. I had time to think about my life and how fast the last two years and one month had passed.

While I was sick at home, I called and made an appointment with Bob Maskmeyer at Conrad Liquor in Afton. I went there and sold myself. I told Maskmeyer that I could do the job. The sales job paid $175 a week. I was taking a big cut, but I was getting out of the cold and messy jobs. I told Willie about the job, and he said I made a good decision. He said the work at the plant would make me old and sick. He couldn't go anywhere because he had been there for twenty-one years and looked forward to retiring.

CHAPTER 29

I started to work at Conrad Liquor Company, and this was good for me. I saw Dory Bolden in the car one day, and I followed him to Birlinda's house. We went into the house, and Birlinda was there with her son. Dory asked about the baby, and she said that her mother was cleaning him up. I never got to see the boy named Harold Moore. Mrs. Davis didn't want me to see him. I talked with Dory, and we made plans to get together. Dory and Delores were married, and Delores was a nurse. The following week, Dory was killed by Delores at home. I went to Dory's family's house and talked and paid my respects. They took his death very hard. It was a big funeral. It made me sad and because of what had happened. I started thinking about what Dory had told me about Mr. Davis's activities and how he didn't like Dory.

The next week after Dory's death, Mr. Leonard C. Davis was killed in the front of his home on Lotus Avenue. I couldn't imagine what would be next. Two families lost loved ones. Birlinda had to come back to St. Louis for her father's funeral. During the funeral, her son was kept by my cousin who lived across the street from the Davis home on Garfield.

My grandmother was visiting with my cousin at the time of the funeral. She noticed that Harold looked like me. So Laura called my mother and told her that she needed to come over and see Birlinda's baby boy. Obine and Josie went to see the baby. When Birlinda returned, Obine invited her to come to dinner the next day. I didn't know about any of this until later. Obine told me that she asked if the boy was my son. Birlinda said no, it wasn't. Obine said that she knew that the boy was mine. Time moved on, and I continued with my education and new job.

30

June Dowell was born. The apartment we lived in was small. I would make the rent on time each month. I was doing well until the rent management company called and asked why I hadn't paid the rent. I explained I had mailed it before the due date. I had to make out the new check and pay a late charge. The next month, it happened again. I went to the office and talked to the manager. He was racist, and I told him so. I called Obine and told her about the rent. She told me to buy a house, because I was a veteran. Obine called one of her old boyfriends, Mr. Chatwell, who was a real estate salesman. I was mad at the rent folks, and I told Chatwell to show me a house. He showed me a small house that had a swimming pool in Moline Acres. Back then, mostly white people lived in that area. I told Willie about the house, and he went over to look at it. He told me that I didn't need a house like that. He suggested a four-family flat so I could make money and still have a place to live.

Chatwell called me one night and said he had a flat I could buy, but we needed to get on it that night. We went to 4960-4962 West Florissant. Chatwell showed me the vacant upstairs apartment. I told him that I would take it. We signed the paper that night. No money down because I was a veteran.

The deal went through, and we moved in a week. I had three white tenants living there. They were paying $40 a month. When I told them I owned the property, they all moved within a month. I cleaned up and painted all the apartments and lay down new carpets in each unit. I rented each unit for $150 per month, with $150 for last month's rent and $50 deposit before tenants could move in. The apartment were rented, and I collected $450 a month, and the note on the building was $200 per month. I added a room to each apartment because we needed the room for June and all her baby stuff.

The building next to mine was for sale, and I bought it. I decorated it myself and fixed it the same. I learned this from Uncle Harvey Raspberry. He owned property. Within a year, I had good money. I paid all the bills, and Betty paid the furniture bills. She bought a green pinto without my permission. Betty would do things like that. I was at home, and a guy and his wife came to our house to get the dining room set. Betty had sold it to them. I let them take it, but it pissed me off. The doorbell, and rang it was Greenbury Furniture with a new dinette set. I signed the paper, and that was that. Betty never said anything about the money she collected. Back then, I should have paid more attention to that because that was the main reason we had problems in our marriage. Betty was slick in all her doings. I was making good money from rent and my job. Betty did what she wanted with her check. I didn't care because I loved her and we had good credit and a lovely daughter.

Betty called me and told me to meet her at this house on 1601 Veronica near the circle. She said this house we could get for $26,000. I told her to call Chatwell, and she had called already. She was always a step ahead of me. Trouble was brewing, and I couldn't see it. We moved and got settled in the new house. Obine came to see the new place, and she didn't stay long because she didn't like Betty.

Life was moving fast now, and Betty was pregnant again. When I graduated from St. Louis University, Betty started back at school, and we needed someone to keep the baby. Mother Brown would keep June every day. She was a nice old lady. She died after about eight months of keeping June. Betty hired another woman, Sister Brown. She came to the house every day. Sister Brown was at our house at 7:00 a.m., and some days she would stay all night. Betty had Teri P. Dowell, and she was born at Christian Hospital on Kingshighway. We were happy with two girls and one car. The job was fine, and I drove a Lincoln continental. I liked that car.

I had been saving government bonds. The man who lived near us came by one day while I was working in the yard and told me he had just bought a new black Lincoln. He came back the next day and showed me his new car. It was beautiful. The guy used to be married to Baby Sister, who had a tavern on Shreve. She was one of my accounts. She was a nice lady, and she would buy new things I had. She was with Bumbstead, who would be in the tavern most of the time. I became friends with her daughter and Lincoln Mark IV. I was real proud of that car. When I went on my route, selling whiskey, the clients started giving me larger orders and getting new items. They were glad to see me excel in the business. Bud Conrad, my boss, called me to the office and asked if I was pimping girls. I found out later why he said that to me. We had two new cars and a new house and a live-in maid for the children. I loved my family and wanted things for them. My cousin Nathaniel Phillips vouched for me, and I became a Master Mason. This was good for me. Nathaniel was like a big brother. He taught me the ropes about the streets and cooled me down. He told me not to argue with people. He told me to listen.

CHAPTER 31

I worked for Conrad Liquor for nine years. All was well. I learned the trade well. Ralph Harris and Archie Roger and I were the only blacks working there. Most of the retailers didn't like Conrad because he wouldn't give them credit cash or COD on delivery. We had the brand names, Cutty Sark, Johnny Walker, _____ Gin, and the wines from Swiss colony out of California. I would win trips and money all the time. Betty and I went to the Kentucky Derby on the company to see Majestic Prince. Life was good. I started playing golf and met many new people. I had good money. Betty wanted a new house, so we moved to 1601 Veronica in St. Louis City. This was a very nice house with three bedrooms and two baths and a nice basement, garage, and yard.

This was when my problems began. As soon as we bought that house, Betty took a turn on the negative end. I worked hard, and her father, Simon Ward, took care of the apartment building for me, painting and maintaining jobs. I paid him, and he did an excellent job for me. I loved Simon; he really respected me and told me down through the years if everyone would stay out on me and marriage we would be together today but she wouldn't listen and Betty had other things on her mind. Working for Conrad was good. I graduated from Saint Louis University, and I gave a copy of my degree to the office manager.

There was a position for a supervisor open, and I applied for it. Bob turned me down and hired Kenneth McGee, a beer salesman, to be over the black salesmen. Kenneth didn't know about the whiskey business, so we had to school him. Ralph Harris left Conrad and went to St. Louis Liquor out.

I wasn't happy with Conrad, especially after I had a degree. I hired Charles Bussy as my attorney. He had graduated from law school and helped me with my personal affairs.

I decided to work on my future. I had a degree in psychology and a minor in business administration. Bussy started me a corporation on paper, where I could go into only business for profit.

The *Daily Record News* published my name in the business records, and the white supervisor Ed Shipper called me to the office and fired me on the spot. I asked him to give me a letter of why they did, and it said I would be a competitor against them. I had only filed corporation paper. I started selling pickles and bar items out of the truck of my car to make ends meet. Betty wasn't happy, and she had a job and didn't help at all.

Bussy helped me file papers for the SBA for a loan of 100,000 for Wm E. Dowell Incorporated. I got a small office and warehouse at 3805-07 Washington to sell goods. My cousin Nath and his son, Marty, would deliver the things we had to sell at night.

I finally got a liquor and wine and beer license to sell to retailer. I was working on a low budget. Sell products and pay bills.

I was still paying bills at the house because I had the rent coming in from the apartments. Betty started being objective to all things I suggested about money. She didn't want to give up any cash. I lived with her for nine years and didn't really know her or about what was coming from her. She would be smiling at me but deceiving me at the same time. We began arguing and not talking. Betty had some of her classmates stop by sometimes, Lloyd Hines and Larry, a policeman for the city, and I became friends with her friend Therman Moore. As things got worse, Betty would leave town for a few days, going to Delta meetings out of town. She was a Delta, and they always were having something.

She came back from one of her trips with Diann, my cousin's wife who lives in East St. Louis. Betty didn't unpack her suitcase and left it open on the bedroom floor. She had gone to work, and I was cleaning up the room and moved the suitcase and noticed a black underwear set, but the panties had a slit in the middle, like some you would buy from a _____ sex store. I had never seen them in it at home. I inspected, and it was soiled with white stuff on the slits.

When she come home, I questioned her about her trip. She played it off as business. Things didn't get any better. I had to hold on to my business, and that's when Nathaniel told me to be patient and not do something I would be sorry for later in my marriage. He told me women were like the wind; they went in different directions daily and think on only one side of the brain, their way.

I came home from work and relaxed at home, waiting for the loan to be approved from the SBA. I called Bussy. He said, "No word yet, it's in the making." I fell asleep and woke up about 10:00 p.m. The wife and children were not here.

I called her mother and asked if they were there or if she had seen them. Lilly Ward said no, she had not. The next day, I went to work at the warehouse, and when I got there, a man was waiting for me to open the business. The man approached me and introduced himself as a process server from the city courts. He gave me a summons for a divorce. Betty had filed, and I didn't know it. Sleeping with her every night and I didn't know. I was hurt and mad now.

CHAPTER 32

Betty and the children were gone for two weeks. While at home, I found unpaid bills, cut-off notices, and past due car note payments from Ford Motor Credit. Betty had the Lincoln Mark V. I called Ford, and they told me they were in the process of coming to get the car. I told the man I would pay, and he said that Betty had been telling them she was sending in the payment but never did. The note was three months behind. I told him I would pay it up. I mailed a check and went to work. When I returned home, the lights were off. She had not paid them. It was dark, and I called; the bills was three months behind. I was in the dark all night. I paid it with a check.

I went to the bank to check our personal account. She had taken that money. Now the checks were gonna bounce. I went to the real estate office that handled the apartment rents and expenses to get the reserve money to cover those checks.

The clerk told me Betty and her lawyer had been there and served the authorized paper to turn over the money. I was bailing now. I called my mother. She gave the money ($5,000) to get me back on my feet. I was gonna pay her back when the SBA loan came.

Two weeks passed. I paid my worker at the business, and I went home about 3:00 p.m. on Friday. I was mentally exhausted with all this and didn't know where my children were. My mother told me the kids were okay and Betty would show.

When I arrived at home, my Lincoln was parked on the street. I took my keys out to open the door, and the key wouldn't unlock. She changed the locks. I could see Lilly Ward, her mother, through the glass. I screamed, "Open the door!" Lilly said, "We don't want no trouble, just go away."

I kept ringing the bell and stayed outside for about twenty minutes, then Betty came to the door and talked through the door. She left and went to the kitchen.

When she came back, I kicked the door in, saying, "This is my house." When I got in, she tried to stab me with a steak knife. I took the knife, and Lilly was pulling us apart. As I stood up, the door was still open, and a white police had his gun pointed at my head.

He said, "I'll blow your head off. Get on the floor." They handcuffed me and took me on the front.

All the neighbors were all out to see what was going on. The sergeant came, and he took the cuffs off me and talked to me and told me that Betty called and that she had a restraining order on me not to be on the property. He told me I could get my belongings and go. I got my guns, clothes, and the Lincoln car.

I went to my mother's house to have a place to stay. I was mad and wanted to hurt Betty. I wanted to hurt her bad; I couldn't sleep.

I called my lawyer, and he said, "Come see me." Before I went to his office, I went by SBA serving office to check on the loan. He told me that they received legal papers from Betty's lawyer, Debensky, to stop the loan because of divorce proceedings.

This was the end for me. I had blood in eyes for Betty Fisher Dowell. I had not seen my children, and she did a job on me.

I got into my car. The next morning, it was running bad. I took it to Ford and left it. Ford called and told me to come back to talk about the car.

The service manager told me that they took the oil pan off and that thumbtacks were in the motor, and it would have to be replaced, plus something in the gas tank wasn't right. I could drive it, but it was gonna stop.

The following week, someone stole the car. The police called me and told me the car was at the salvage yard on Broadway and I could get it there.

The car was titled in Betty's name, so I couldn't get it. I called Betty and told her what happened. She agreed to have it taken to

East St. Louis, close to my mother's home. I called the insurance man, and he called me and told me he would get on it.

Two weeks passed. I went to the dealer about the car, and they told me that Betty and her lawyer removed the car to Hill Top Ford in St. Louis. Slick Betty got me again. Her and that lawyer; she had been sleeping with him too. They got me again.

The insurance man called me and told me that Betty and the lawyer were trying to get all the money because the car was titled, but my name was on the policy.

He warned me if the check didn't have the two signatures on it, they wouldn't honor it.

Betty called to meet at the bank. She gave half the money. I took it and left. Months rolled by, and Betty moved in Barbara, her woman from New York, in the house. Yes, this was the problem all along. She was gay, still is today. We divorced, and I moved on. She tried to get the money for back child support. Things reversed on Betty for fraud by getting relief for June and Teri while they were emancipated from home. Getting welfare benefit while the girls were not living with her, she still paying the states according to the lawyer. I could go on with the other bad stuff she did with Larry the cop, but that was on them. Bad luck to ya'll. It's coming to you before death. That lawyer (white) too; Betty is still alone with no one and sick.

CHAPTER 33

I never got the loan. I closed the corporation and opened up a new life.

I married Marilyn Colmen, and we had one child together, Dr. Jessica Dowell Brown. I opened the Butter Rump tripe back in 1979 but closed it in 1984 due to a fire. We raised Leslie, Marcano Jr., and Jessica at 5944 Kenney, where I was the Republican committee man for four years.

Marilyn and I divorced back in 1993, and I took Jessica and raised her on my own. Marilyn I loved but couldn't live with because of her habits and drinking. I really loved her, but I had to leave, or I would be locked up for murder or dead back then. Marilyn passed away. We had good memories to cherish. She told me before her death that I was the best man she ever had and that she messed up and things couldn't be fixed. While crying, she kissed me and said she was sorry. Marilyn died the next day.

I'm married to Shirley Washington Dowell, a wonderful woman who has been my pillow of strength to overcome all obstacles in life. She is responsible for our achievements and trusts in my judgment on everything.

A lot a things went bad in my life, but more good overshadowed the bad and, it was the experience of these events that I caution my children and grandchildren about because I had been there, and they would be coming to those pitfalls in life.

Love of life brings second, third, fourth chances to start over again for the good.

Bill and Flash

William Dowell and Dr. Jessica Dowell

William Dowell/Dr. Jessica K. Dowell-Teri Dowell

Jessica, Wm. Teri Dowell

Shirley Dowell, Obine Dowell Williams

Shirley and William Dowell

Wallace M. Green Jr.

Terri Dowell

Terri   Jessica   Morgan

Morgan

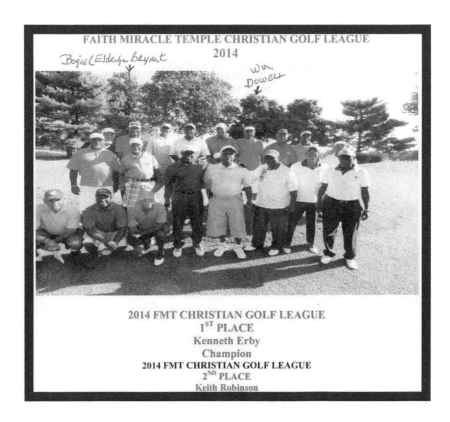

FAITH MIRACLE TEMPLE CHRISTIAN GOLF LEAGUE
2014

Bogie (Eldridge Bryant

Wm. Dowell

2014 FMT CHRISTIAN GOLF LEAGUE
1ST PLACE
Kenneth Erby
Champion
2014 FMT CHRISTIAN GOLF LEAGUE
2ND PLACE
Keith Robinson

2014 FMT CHRISTIAN GOLF LEAGUE
3RD PLACE
Marlon Baylor

2014 FMT CHRISTIAN GOLF LEAGUE
4TH PLACE
Jeffrey Taylor

2014 FMT CHRISTIAN GOLF LEAGUE
5TH PLACE
Elliot Coleman

2014 FMT CHRISTIAN GOLF LEAGUE
6TH PLACE
James Wade

2014 FMT CHRISTIAN GOLF LEAGUE
7TH PLACE
Ronald Neal

2014 FMT CHRISTIAN GOLF LEAGUE
8TH PLACE
Jimmy Riddle

ABOUT THE AUTHOR

If William Dowell said it, it's true and full of integrity. He means what he says. His word is good. If he says he is going to do something for you, bet on it.

9 781683 480303